Conten P9-DIY-813

contents

Google+

Peripherals

Index

Introduction

Social media exists because of our collected desire to stay connected; not just to the people we know, but to the things we like. It's a way to announce our successes and share our discoveries. It's where people turn for breaking news and viral videos. Social media has become a major means of spreading information between people, across countries and cultures, and it's only becoming more important.

From the outside, it's easy to dismiss social media as just another distraction to your already jam-packed daily routine. But actually, social media can create the opposite effect. Instead of having to reach out in many directions to stay connected, social media helps you keep track of your friends, family and interests all in the same place. You can use your accounts to find out who's just had a baby or landed a new job, and just as easily check in on world news or the latest injury report from your favourite team. And that process works in both directions – sharing updates and interests to your social media accounts helps your connections keep up to date with what's been going on in your life.

There is, of course, more than one social media service out there (hence the many chapters in this book). They can be used in various ways – Facebook as a scrapbook, Twitter for instant alerts, LinkedIn to pip someone to a job – and you can join as few or many as your needs demand. You may take to one more than another, though if you're completely new to social media you should probably start with Facebook. It's currently the biggest service of its kind and just about everyone, and everything, is on it already. Once you have a sense of what Facebook provides, you'll better appreciate the unique features of its competitors.

As you explore the world of social media, think back upon your first experiences with the web. Remember the thrill of uncovering the new and the unusual, the sort of things you'd have never found if left disconnected. Social media is another step forward in sharing information, making it both more personal and more immediate. It's a field that will continue to evolve, rapidly, and in response to the very ways in which we use it.

About this book

The Rough Guide to Social Media for Beginners explains the first steps involved in engaging with social media. It starts with a basics section that tackles common misconceptions and fears associated with social networking. Subsequent chapters (roughly in order of current popularity) introduce the big social networks and explain how to use them, along with the chief benefits of doing so. In addition to Facebook and Twitter, we also cover the more career-orientated LinkedIn and explain why newcomers Google+ and Tumblr are well worth a look. The final chapter touches upon some smaller social media channels, and shares some of the best add-ons to help you round out your social networking experience. Though we've not been able to cover every facet of every site, we've aimed to give you the tools and confidence you'll need to explore the exciting world of social media on your own.

The web changes at breakneck speed. While we've tried to be as accurate as possible with information throughout, a social media service may have changed its appearance or added new features between the time this book was written and you started reading it. In general, changes within services – like bug fixes – are often minor, and you can easily overlook them without your experience being impacted in the least. But when a service adjusts its interface, the changes may seem more dramatic (even if they're actually cosmetic and all the usual features and functions remain available). This latter case may cause some confusion when trying to reconcile what you see on the screen with images in this book. If you're at a complete loss, locate the help page for that service, and type what you're looking for into their query field. They'll find it for you and provide some information as to how it may work differently than you'd expected.

Text written like **this** indicates a command as it appears on a computer or mobile phone screen. Something written like **this** denotes key terms and emphasizes areas where you'll find specific controls.

The Basics

The Basics

Where we put the horse
before the cart

General questions

What is social media?

Simply put, it's a way for groups of people to come together on the Internet where they can share ideas and opinions. There have been numerous takes on exactly how people might get together online, and many tools developed to help us share what we've seen and heard. As social media has become more mature some favourites have risen to the top, including **Facebook**, **Twitter**, **LinkedIn** and **Google+**. They all have their own strengths and weaknesses, and later on in the book we'll describe how each might best suit your needs.

How has this all come about?

It's been suggested that we humans naturally exist in tribes. Blame it on our furry ancestors, huddling around each

Social media extends your reach through strong to weak connections, making it possible to find new friends who share your interests. This connectivity pathway can also be used to promote a product, business or organization.

other for warmth and protection. Of course, this sort of behaviour requires us to be pretty near one another, and for millennia our tribes have been largely defined by where we live.

Leap forward to the age of telephones, satellites and the Internet, and we start to hear about something called the **global village**. We're no longer restricted to tribes we can reach out and touch; now we can interact with anyone, anywhere, just as quickly as if they were in the hut next door. It seems inevitable that we'd end up using our amazing modern communications technology to organize ourselves into new tribes, but this time they're based on our interests rather than how close together our homes may be.

Is this the end of civilization as we know it?

It's extremely unlikely that we'll completely abandon our neighbours for keyboards and online video. And we'll certainly never escape our real-life connections to family and friends (as much as we may sometimes want to do just that). What social media has given us is the ability to meet people from all over the **planet**, people who share our own interests who we'd otherwise have never known existed.

What's in it for me?

Contact. At the most basic level, social media lets us stay in touch with the people we know and the things we like. Having an account with Facebook or LinkedIn or one of the other tools out there creates an amazing number of possible interactions. You might simply want to keep track of your children, or you may want to promote a business or find a

 new job. Engaging with social media can give you a whole new handle on the world around you.

Is social media the same as blogging?

Well before the Facebooks and Twitters of the world, there was an explosion of online diary-keeping called blogging. The idea of sharing your thoughts and pictures with other people is core to the **social** side of social media, and the early blog movement was key to the invention of the services that are so popular today. Later in the book we'll take a look at **Tumblr** – a popular **microblog** that sits somewhere between blogs and the services that evolved from them.

Is it safe?

It's as safe as any interaction you have with anyone in the real world. Safer even, since there's very little risk of you being injured by some random madman while sitting in the comfort of your own home. Remember, though, the rules of civility apply online as well.

Do I have to pay?

Not for entry-level service, and that often includes just about every feature you'll want to use. There are **add-ons** and other helpful options from **third-party companies** that will ask for a fee, and there are a number of games that draw you in with a limited version, only to suggest you splash

These organizations verify that a business is real and has sufficient checks in place to safeguard your credit information.

some cash on an upgrade. It's entirely up to you, and we'll suggest some of the better choices if you're looking to spend.

Can someone steal my money, or my identity?

There are definite risks out there, but if you apply the same common-sense approach you take when out shopping or travelling, the odds turn entirely in your favour. You wouldn't write your personal identification details and credit card numbers on a piece of paper and tack it up on a coffee house wall, nor would you invite complete strangers to dig through your wallet. Only share your personal or financial details if you trust the person or company you're giving them to.

Do I have to use my real name?

While you might use social media to reinvent yourself online, harsh reality will inevitably come knocking. Being honest about your information is the first step towards **connecting** with people who like the things that you like, and

you'll find you ultimately get more when you give more. Of course, this doesn't mean that you can't glam yourself up with a clever **Twitter** handle (see p.114) or have some fun setting up a farcical Facebook group.

facebook

Can this onion ring get more fans than Justin Bieber?

It did, by more than a million votes (and counting).

How am I supposed to know whom to trust?

You'll need to gain some social media experience before you can confidently flush out the fakes from the genuine articles. Some **scams** may be obvious, but others not so much. Certainly avoid strangers bearing gifts, but sometimes friends can be just as dangerous. Just because you receive a request from a friend to download a particular file or application doesn't mean it's a safe thing to do. Sometimes your friends have had their accounts **hacked**, and other times they just don't pay attention to what they're sending on. If you have any doubt, contact the person who sent you the request and ask them what it's all about.

TIP: Facebook offers a quick overview of the do's and don'ts of online security that you can apply to all your online interactions: http://www.facebook.com/security

What if someone hacks my account?

On very rare occasions, hackers may figure out your password and send **spam** to all of your contacts, or sign you up for all sorts of mailing lists you would never think to join. They may have been able to crack the code because your password was too simple, or they may have found a way into your account through an application or add-on that you'd inadvertently accepted. Though

16

annoying, it's usually harmless, and every social media site will provide some way to verify and **regain control** over your account.

Will people bully or harass me?

There have been serious cases of **cyberbullying** over the years, and the very public nature of the web can quickly intensify feelings of shame or loneliness. While it is much more common to hear reports of children being bullied, that hasn't stopped such behaviour from entering the professional and personal world of adults. If you or your  child find yourself being harassed, consult an expert at www.wiredsafety.org. They can help you figure out an appropriate response to the situation, which may include installing monitoring software like www.spectorsoft.com that will record everything that comes and goes through your computer.

Can everyone see everything I'm doing?

People will know as much about you as you're willing to let them know. While many default settings for social media programs often make your movements and comments open to everyone, you can **refine** and **filter** who sees what. But remember, YOU are your own finest filter. If you decide to put information about your thoughts, feelings or actions on the web, it will be seen. Consider what you're saying and how you want to be perceived before posting.

It's online, does it really matter what I say?

You may feel like there's some buffer between your online and real-world personas, but over the last decade the two have pretty much become the same thing. If you're just getting started in the whole social media arena, don't enter guns blazing – to start, **caution** is the keyword. You shouldn't put everything out there all at once. Ease into it. You wouldn't walk into a room full of friends and strangers and loudly pronounce your religious and political views, and you probably shouldn't do that online either. Civility extends to the web, too. The planet has gotten smaller, not less well behaved.

Proper spelling and grammar are encouraged online, though some shorthand is acceptable (see p.140).

Amy Kahmille Ardito
after doing my maths problems last night i feel like i just concord something huge, i feel so accomplished!!
29 minutes ago · Like · Comment

 Tim Sacco likes this.

Alyssa Morris Have you done your English homework yet?
2 minutes ago · Like

How much is too much?

That really depends on the particular flavour of social media you're using. It's not uncommon to fire off five or ten **tweets** in a day (see p.123), but equalling that with Facebook status changes is a sure way to annoy friends and followers. Similarly, constantly adjusting your **LinkedIn** profile makes you look unstable, whereas rating loads of books on **Goodreads** (see p.263) may come across as impressive (though possibly a bit showy).

Will this affect my job?

There have been plenty of reports about how a Facebook or Twitter post has resulted in fines or punishment (including firing). Remember, anything you put online is up there for good, because even if you take it down there's a chance someone could access a saved version of the offending communiqué. An "I'm so drunk" caption alongside a racy photo is probably not the sort of thing you want coming back to visit just before your next job review. Sharing your foolish or obnoxious exploits can also keep you from landing a new job elsewhere, as it is now common practice for potential employers to check your social media presence during the interview stages.

> God this fairtrade, organic banana is shit. Can I have a slave-grown, chemically enhanced, genetically modified one please?
> 9:02 AM Jul 8th, 2009 via TweetDeck
>
> **stuartmaclennan**
> Stuart MacLennan

Once an up-and-comer in the Labour Party, Stuart MacLennan tweeted himself right out of the running.

Can it help me in my current job?

Actually, yes! Having an understanding of how social media works is a definite advantage in the job market. Companies the world over are putting more eggs in the social media basket, and without at least some understanding of how the threads tie together you'll find yourself behind the pack. But don't fret, using social media as a business tool is a young science, and you'll be able to get up to speed in no time at all (see p.98).

What about finding work?

There are sites whose very existences are based on helping people find new jobs (see p.179), but every group you join, on any site, creates innumerable networking possibilities.

Sites like www.99designs. com use **crowdsourcing** to match graphic artists with design projects.

Seasoned professionals use social media to keep track of contacts they hope to work with in the future. Freelancers point to online **portfolios** to showcase their skills. Entrepreneurs band together to turn side projects into full-fledged businesses. With all this connectivity, you're only limited by your own drive and ingenuity.

What about my home business?

Social media is amazingly useful for small and home businesses. With a little bit of effort up front, you can develop an online presence that makes your tiny basement startup feel like a legitimate commercial enterprise. If you can convey the same sense of care to your online audience as you give your in-the-flesh customers, you may well find yourself with a very popular business. It won't happen overnight, and it will require you to check in with some regularity, but thanks to some very clever services none of it seems that much like work. We'll go into it more fully later on (see p.143).

Wiggly Wigglers, a gardening business in Herefordshire, maintains a blog, Facebook group, Twitter account and YouTube channel. Winner of numerous small business awards, theirs is a model worth emulating.

Whatever happened to word of mouth?

It's moved online. Social media is a powerful tool for generating **buzz**, and it's even better at providing a forum for satisfied (or dissatisfied) customers. While you'd never begrudge a customer for recommending you to her friends, a five-star review on the web can make a broader impact. And thanks to the very public nature of social media, you can dip in on the conversation, as long as you invite your customers to a place where they can share their opinions and experiences (see p.98).

What if I head a club or cause?

Small organizations bought in to the benefits of social media very early on, first for broadcasting messages among

21

members, and then as a place for conversation. Using the simplest features, you'll be able to alert everyone to changes in schedule, share updates on goals, organize **events** or poll the group while working towards consensus (see p.53).

How do I join?

The only requirement is an **email address**. Any one will do, though it's a good idea to separate your professional accounts from your personal ones. Most of us have an email account by now, but if you don't, or you rely entirely on your work account, you should probably try the offerings from Google or Yahoo! for home use. A Google mail account has the added advantage of tying directly in with their social media platform Google+ (see p.207).

▶ **Gmail** mail.google.com

▶ **Yahoo!** mail.yahoo.com

Which site should I join?

There are a lot of different sites out there, and they can coexist because each addresses a different need (though there is a lot of crossover). Of the major players, **Facebook** is the most popular, and is used for both connecting with friends and promoting businesses; **Twitter** is a simple way to learn about breaking news; and **Google+** is a mixture of both. Small but powerful, **Tumblr** is a highly customizable blog service, and **LinkedIn** is all about advancing your career.

What sort of computer will I need?

If you purchased a computer in the last five years, you should be just fine. Social media is primarily web-based, so as long as you can run the latest web **browsers**, you'll be able to see and hear everything social media has to offer. Plus, using the latest browsers provides the tightest security for your online experience. Older computers will work too, though you're likely to experience some lag when trying to watch videos or listen to audio clips.

What web browser should I use?

Any modern web browser will work, and by modern we mean updated within the last year. Currently, **Firefox**, **Internet Explorer**, and **Google Chrome** are the most popular web browsers, followed by **Safari** and **Opera**. Any of these will work, though some experts have expressed concern about Internet Explorer's stability and security. If you have a Windows PC, you'll already have Internet Explorer. If you run with the Macintosh crowd, Safari will come standard.

- ▶ **Firefox** www.mozilla.com
- ▶ **Chrome** www.google.com/chrome
- ▶ **Opera** www.opera.com

Will it work on my mobile phone?

That depends on what type of phone you have. Most **smartphones** are able to connect to Facebook, Twitter and the rest by way of **apps** – little programs that make navigating social media sites easier on the small screen. Really, though, all you need is web access on your phone, and you can sign

in to your accounts just as you do on your computer. The less "smart" your phone is, the less likely you'll be able to use it for your social media accounts, especially when **tagging** your location in status updates and photos you take.

The Facebook app for the iPhone reorganizes the page to better fit the phone's screen, making it easier to stay up to date while on the move.

Facebook

Facebook

The biggest of them all

If you delve no further into the world of social media than Facebook, you'll have done plenty. Facebook boasts more than 750 million active users, so chances are you'll discover whomever or whatever you're looking for within its virtual walls. Its constantly expanding array of features will have you tweaking this and adjusting that both in the near and long terms, all while making new friends, chatting online, sharing pictures and videos, playing games, expressing your joy (or anger) – even developing a business presence and building ad campaigns.

Underneath all the polish, Facebook is essentially an informal information network, a place you can go to find out about old classmates or pose a question to a mass audience. It makes us feel more connected to the people we know and the things we like, without actually having to get up and see them every time we want to check in. It can help us meet people and discover new ideas, or force us to confront long-standing beliefs. All of this from a service that started out in a college dormitory!

Sign me up

Creating a personal Facebook account is a straightforward affair (we'll discuss business accounts a bit later, see p.98). Head to www.facebook.com and give them your email address and birth date. Work out a strong password that's easy to remember (see tip below), then fill in a few personal details, upload a photo and start finding your friends. There are tons of places to explore and options to adjust, but at the start the best thing you can do is just throw yourself into it.

Prove who you are

Providing a valid email address is really the only prohibitive safeguard that Facebook has in place, and once you sign up for an account they'll send a confirmation email to the address you've provided. It's a good idea to use a **personal email account** for signing up, rather than your professional one. If you don't have a personal email account, we've suggested a few at the start of the book (see p.22). Until you get the hang of who-sees-what inside Facebook, it's best to keep your home and work worlds separate. You can bring them together down the road if necessary.

> **TIP:** A strong password will contain a combination of uppercase and lowercase letters, numbers and symbols. It should have no connection to any personal data (e.g. your name or address). The best consist of more than one word jammed together in some unlikely fashion.

You'll want to provide an accurate birth date, too. For one, Facebook will use your age to determine whether certain pages or pieces of content are age-appropriate. It will also automatically alert all your friends to your birthday (you can hide the year, see p.33).

Security Check

Enter both words below, separated by a space.
Can't read the words below? Try different words or an audio captcha.

Woodruff ~~RptiCH~~

Text in the box: [   ] What's this?

Submit Cancel

CAPTCHA: Completely Automated Public Turing test to tell Computers and Humans Apart

The final step of the identity verification process is identifying the garbled letters in a CAPTCHA test. This is to keep out devious hackers and their computerized **bots** – programs created to acquire thousands of accounts for the sole purpose of **spamming** people from the inside. You're never given the clearest selection of letters and numbers, and even the audio option can be confusing, but you'll have more than one chance at passing in the event you mistype.

First contacts

Facebook – like just about every service we'll cover in this book – will ask for access to your email address book. Though on the surface this seems intrusive, they won't keep

☑ Select All Friends

Beware of blindly requesting everyone Facebook identifies as a potential friend.

your password information and you'll save yourself hours of manually searching for people you already know on Facebook. The whole process takes less than a minute, and you're presented with a list of everyone whose email address you've saved. But be careful about sending out a **mass invite** to everyone who has been automatically identified – many email services will save the address of anyone you've ever corresponded with, meaning you could end up reaching out to people who you barely know, or to people you're no longer friends with.

You're not limited to searching your online email contacts. Facebook will happily pick through any address book saved  on your computer, and if you have a **Skype** account – a brilliant program that enables voice and video chats online – they'll search that too. They'll even give you the option of sending an invite to anyone in your list who hasn't already registered with Facebook.

A touch of detail

You'll have the chance to proclaim all your likes and interests a little later on (see p.37), but for now Facebook just wants to know where you went to school and where you've worked. Facebook was originally limited to university students (the company took its name from the headshot booklets given to incoming first years), and that remains one of the quickest ways to identify people you may know. **Work**, the other major thread in all of our lives, can offer even more potential friends. But the most tempting place to look is under your high school listings. Here's where Facebook will uncover all those old classmates from your hometown and give you the chance to reconnect.

Facebook is never satisfied with adding one friend per sitting, always suggesting more potential connections whenever you add a new one.

Requesting even one friend from a former school or workplace sets off a chain reaction in Facebook. As soon as you hit "send request", you're presented with a slew of other people you may know. The suggestions can be surprisingly accurate, as Facebook searches through not only your contacts, but friends of your friends with whom you have some overlap. They'll even highlight people who have searched for you, and occasionally use a combination of your age and location history to pull options seemingly out of thin air.

Smile for the camera

After telling Facebook about yourself, it's time to show them what you look like. Your default photo will be a featureless, though gender-appropriate icon. Cold and demanding, it's there to encourage you to get a photo in place before you go any further.

There's no rule that says you must use a headshot for your **profile pic**, but since you're trying to find people who know you, your face should be considered a genuine selling point. There are plenty of ways to adjust photos to fit Facebook's requirements (see p.68), but at the start simply find a good snapshot of yourself on your computer and use Facebook's **thumbnail**

Facebook's Tintin-esque placeholder reminds us to get our own pic up, pronto.

tool to highlight your head. Your home page will display the full version of the picture, but whenever you send requests or make comments on another person's page, it's your thumbnail that's attached.

Filling in the details

While Facebook churns in the background, calculating new friend suggestions and figuring out what ads to hit you with, you might take some time to flesh out your **profile**. Accessed by way of the **about** and **like** buttons on your **timeline** (see p.60), this information will make it easier to find the people and things you like, and for the people and things you like to find you.

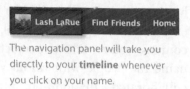

The navigation panel will take you directly to your **timeline** whenever you click on your name.

Basic information

Though you may think you've already sketched out the most general picture of who you are during the sign-up process, there are a few more identifying features that are immediately relevant. Namely, what **languages** you speak and whether you're looking for a romantic relationship. Here, too, is where you can hide the part of your birth date you may have been protecting: your **birth year**. Your friends will still receive an alert

History by Year

2012	Worked at DK Publishing
	Worked at Rough Guides
2000	Worked at Oxford University Press, UK
1993	Went to St. Augustine Prep

Your **about** page includes a brief history of your employment and schooling. You can change what's displayed by adjusting your work and education information (see overleaf).

when it's your birthday (see p.53), they just won't know exactly how old you are.

Work and education

Yes, you were prompted to provide some information about your schooling and employment history at the start, but Facebook would really like to know every place you've ever worked or gone to school. They also suggest you list **courses** you've taken, **projects** you've worked on and name the people with whom you've **collaborated**. In addition, projects and courses give you space to include detailed descriptions of your research and responsibilities, and choose a date range for your involvement.

Facebook uses a pop-up feature to help you find people who may have been with you on your school/work journey, but only if they're already your Facebook friend. Anyone else requires an email address, which Facebook hopes to link with a current member. Once identified, that person will be sent an **alert**, giving them the chance to confirm your association.

Featured friends (in this case, People of Brooklyn) always get top billing on your profile page.

People of Brooklyn (6)

Suman Ganguli
Cornell

Clara Kim

Audrey Lynn Weston
Columbia

Friends (223)

Brendan Higgins

Sonia Choi Pak

Peter Grasse

Peter Labella
Oxford University

All about you

Many of us will have signed up for a Facebook account ages ago, but never bothered filling in all our details. What's the point, after all? Well, besides helping Facebook find new things you might like, you'll be creating a sort of personal advertisement that lets potential connections identify you. Communities form around shared interests, whether they be football, knitting or politics. You don't need to fill in every profile field, or any for that matter, but letting other people know where your interests lie is one of the best ways to spark new friendships.

Relationships and family

Though there may be more you want to keep from your family than share with them, don't count them out completely – they might just become an integral part of your Facebook experience. Facebook happily provides a way to link up with your family members, even going so far as to help you remember their relation to you. Simply type in their names, and if they're currently your Facebook friends they'll pop up in a list of suggestions. In the event that you're not already friends, you can provide Facebook with an email address and an invitation will be sent at once.

TIP: Change Facebook's display language from English to one of over 70 possibilities (including pirate) by clicking on the language option at the very bottom of your home screen.

Philosophy

If explaining yourself in the About Me section wasn't completely satisfying, Facebook goes deeper, asking the sort of things you're not supposed to talk about in polite conversation. Starting with your **religious** and **political** views, Facebook continues mining your personality by having you select your **heroes** – it's actually a very open system, and though they have thousands of suggestions waiting to pop open as you type, Facebook will let you write anything you want into these fields. And don't feel pressured to fill out every last detail – you can return to this

For a pithy saying, www.BrainyQuotes. com is a great source – and their half-million Facebook fans would probably agree.

page whenever you'd like to revise and update. As a last step you'll be given some space to provide a favourite **quotation**. As with every other part of your profile, everyone will see what you've written unless you adjust your privacy settings accordingly.

People Who Inspire You: Who inspires you?

Grigori Rasputin | Euclid | Macho Man Randy | Chairman Mao | Joan of Arc

The globe icon is your pathway to privacy (see p.74).

Arts and entertainment

Finally, we've made it to the fun stuff – though people may scrutinize your taste in film just as closely as your political views. Caveats aside, tapping into our leisurely pursuits has a way of bringing the whole space to life. You can't redesign the Facebook site (like you can with Tumblr, see p.152), so

"Like" buttons are scattered all over the web.

your details are how you'll show a bit of individuality. And in many ways, your interests can better define you than your philosophy.

Facebook wants to link you with the things you like just as much as it wants to connect you with the people you know. When you select one of the suggested drop-down items, you automatically **like** it, whether it be a musician, book, film, TV show or game. So whenever any of your "likes" update their status, you'll be alerted in your **news feed** (see p.42). Want to know if your favourite band is coming to town? Not sure when

the next instalment of that epic fantasy series is set for release? You'll find out straight from the source.

Television:	eas
	BBC EastEnders
	Kenny Powers of Eastbound & Down
	Clint Eastwood
	East Enders
	Eastbound and Down
	Eastwick
	Borongan, Eastern Samar
	eas

Drop-down menus full of possible "likes" spring into action at your first keystroke.

Sports

Sports teams often have very active and vocal followers. We hear supporters in the terraces and in the pubs, and now they have the Internet to raise their voices across. Facebook would like to know if you **play** or **follow** any sport, and they also suggest marking down a few key athletes from your "best-of" list.

As you add your preferences, you'll be simultaneously signing up to hear from them in your news feed, but you'll also be helping Facebook refine its suggestions for groups or people you may want to join or follow. If you've marked down shuffleboard under sports, Facebook is more likely to suggest you join appropriate organizations in your area instead of prompting you to follow Australian Rules football.

Facebook's sponsored links are designed specifically for you, based on your location, age, gender and stated preferences.

Activities and interests

Just in case you've missed sharing the details about some small part of your personality, Facebook provides one last chance to fill in the cracks. You may find that you'll return to these fields more often than the others, as your general likes tend to evolve more quickly than, say, your philosophy.

> **Tip:** You can remove individual suggestions from Facebook's sponsored links by hovering your mouse over the link until an "×" pops up, and then clicking it.

Secure your contact information

While you may want to leave some elements of your Facebook **profile** open for all to see, letting any random stranger access the information on your contact page could be annoying, and possibly downright dangerous. Yes, you can provide an **email address** and **phone number**, even your address and **instant messenger** account name, but do not make them accessible to the public. Letting people get in touch with you outside the confines of Facebook can be very useful, but you should carefully consider who's worthy of the privilege.

By default, the fields on your contact information screen are set to allow only your friends full access. But, as in the real world, you'll inevitably have some friends who are closer than others. Fortunately, there are ways to refine who can see what for just about every part of your Facebook profile (see p.74).

Facebook's first line of defence against unwelcome requests: the privacy drop-down menu.

Finding friends

Facebook has an official credit system in place (see p.97), but friends are the real currency on the site. Filling in your personal details will help Facebook suggest new connections, and while those suggestions can be quite accurate, you'll probably want to take a more active role in the process.

Facebook suggests

When you first sign up for Facebook, you'll be asked to identify friends from your email contacts (see p.29). You will likely already know a good number of people with Facebook accounts, and inviting them to be friends can be as easy as clicking a button. But if you haven't a load of contacts currently signed up, or if you don't want to send out invitations right away, Facebook gives you the chance to reconsider whenever

you sign in. Admittedly, this prompt can try your patience, and it simply won't go away until you add enough friends, upload enough photos (see p.65) and write enough status updates (see p.44) to convince Facebook you've gotten the hang of it all.

Whenever you find yourself on your **home page** (see p. 42),

Homepage friend suggestions are ever-present, but you can delete poor choices by hovering your mouse over the person, and clicking the ✕ that pops up.

you'll see a box on the right dedicated to connecting you with people you may know. Facebook mines your work and location data to find candidates, and uses your present connections as a link to new ones. As you add friends, you create a web of interconnectivity that will produce more accurate friend suggestions.

> **TIP:** You uploaded your contacts to Facebook, but now you want them back. Head to www.facebook.com/contact_importer/remove_uploads.php and choose **remove**. You'll still receive friend suggestions, though they may now be a little further off the mark.

Friend finder

A more elegant tool for finding friends is Facebook's **friend finder**, a service that resides on the other side of your friends bookmark in your timeline (see p.60). After clicking the bookmark, you'll see a **find friends** icon in the upper right. Behind that is a highly refinable list of conditions that will help focus in on a particular group of people you may know. Choosing some combination of your hometown, current location, education and employment history can uncover potential friends with an amazing degree of precision.

Have you been poked? Poking is the Facebook way of letting someone know you're thinking about them, without requiring the thought needed for crafting a full message. You can **poke** friends by going to their timeline page, clicking the **gear icon** next to message, and choosing poke.

Home

When you log in to Facebook, you're taken directly to your home page. On the right is the **ticker** (see p.48), the **bookmarks sidebar** is on the left (see p.52), and smack dead in the centre of the screen is the news feed – a running scroll of all the things happening in your Facebook world. If someone's changed their relationship status or if they have something to say about the latest news cycle, it'll show up here. The more Facebook friends and likes you have, the more updates you'll see. You're also given the option of posting updates about your own comings and goings, sharing photos and videos, and posing questions to the masses (all of which will be copied back to your timeline, see p.60).

News feeds

When your friends write new posts, you'll see what they're saying in your **news feed**. Taking into consideration who you most frequently interact with, Facebook marks some of your friend's posts as **top stories** and promotes them to the top of your feed. Sometimes they get it right, sometimes they're a bit off.

Top stories in your news feed are highlighted with a blue triangle.

To help Facebook better determine who you most want to hear more from, simply click the upper left corner of a post to change its top news status.

Please, no more

On occasion, someone you've befriended stops being your friend, whether because of some real-world breakup or because they simply won't stop filling your news feed with inane updates. If you've had a serious falling out, chances are you'll want to delete the person from your friend list, and maybe even **block them** (see p.77) so they can't find you in a search. But what if you don't want to be so overt with your dismissal? And maybe you're not quite ready to cut ol' blabbermouth out of your life *completely*…

Adjusting your **subscription** preferences will let you silence a friend's feed, while leaving them none the wiser. Hover your mouse over any of their updates in your news feed, then click the tiny arrow that appears in the upper right-hand corner. From there you can choose how much you want to hear from that person.

> Mark as top story
> Hide story
> Report story or spam
>
> Subscribed to Joseph
> All Updates
> ✓ **Most Updates**
> Only Important
>
> Unsubscribe from activity stories by Joseph
> Unsubscribe from Joseph

In the event that you mend fences, or decide that person might not be quite so unbearable anymore, you can always reinstate them to your wall by editing your news feed preferences. Hover your mouse over **news feed** in your sidebar (see p.52) and then click the pen icon that pops up. From there you can add the once-banished back into the mix.

News Feed

Once past the top stories, Facebook posts a mishmash of updates from friends, family and organizations. If you'd rather see what's happening with specific groups of friends, you can refine the news feed using the **lists** Facebook made from the personal

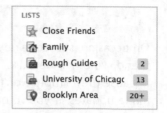

Facebook keeps track of the number of new posts in each list since the last time you checked.

details you've provided. These lists live on the left side of your screen inside the **bookmarks sidebar** (you can also create your own lists by hand, see p.52). Clicking a list will change your feed so it only includes posts from friends in that list.

Updating your status

Checking in on what your friends are doing is only part of the equation. The news feed is also where your personal musings are displayed for all your friends to see – unless you decide to share with a smaller, or larger, group of people.

Clicking on **update status** opens a new window where you're encouraged to jot down your thoughts. You're also given the opportunity to tag whom you're with and where you are, and to control who can see your **post**. And you're

Say something about this link...

You must've had a reason for copying and pasting that link into your status – Facebook will nudge you for an explanation, and your friends will appreciate you for it.

not limited to reporting only that which flows naturally from your fingers – copying a link to an online story will automatically fill your status with a short description and an accompanying picture for that link.

Beyond mere words, your status can contain photos and video, or you could pose a question to part or all of the Facebook community. Holding off on the photos for now (see p.65), the questions feature can be both fun and informative. Not only can you create open queries, you can click **Ask Question** and design a **poll** that will restrict possible answers to a multiple choice selection. Not sure if you should head to St Lucia, the Azores or the Dalmatian coast for your next vacation? Poll your friends, they're sure to have an opinion!

Polls can be commented upon and shared, or answers can be left open so friends can suggest new choices.

Commenting and sharing

You will, on occasion, find a friend's status particularly worthy of your response. Whether you agree or disagree with what they've posted, there are ways to express your opinion of their opinion. You may want to provoke further discussion (or derail it), pass the thread along to someone outside the conversation, or you may simply want to show your support without getting too involved. Whatever the case, Facebook has you covered.

The least involved you can be without ignoring the post ⬆️ Like · Comment · Share · completely is to hit the **like** button. This tiny act sends an alert to your friend's ticker, letting her know you've thrown your support her way. And considering the sort of responses some people write after opening up a **comment** box, collecting likes is sometimes preferable.

You can also **share** posts – though only when your friends have copied a web link into their status. Sharing will expand the original post on your friend's wall to

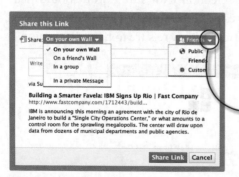

Privacy options apply to sharing just as they do to your posts and personal information.

acknowledge everyone who has passed along the link. It will also post the link to your timeline as your own status, or let you share it to a friend's timeline, to a group (see p.53) or via private message, while providing space to add your personal thoughts on the matter.

TIP: Facebook will send you an email when new comments are added to a post on which you've previously commented.

Subscriptions

From time to time, your friends will share posts that originate from outside your friend list. Assuming they've grabbed your attention, you might try to bridge the gap and "friend" that third party yourself. But if you're satisfied with your current friendships and aren't interested in letting more people have access to your timeline, you can still receive updates from non-friends by simply **subscribing** to their posts. Find your way to the page of the person you'd like to hear more from, and click **subscribe**.

Subscriptions let you fine tune the kind of updates you see (from friends and people you only follow).

From now on you'll see all of that person's public comments within your own news feed.

Subscriptions work the same way in both directions, so people you don't know can tune in to your witty and poignant take on life – but only if you enable subscriptions on

While spam is always a concern, leaving yourself open to new friendships is sometimes worth the hassle.

your account, and then only for status posts you make **public** (this sort of asymmetric relationship is very much like following someone on Twitter, see p.132). To let people follow your public posts, head to www.facebook.com/about/subscribe and hit the green **allow subscribers** button. From there you can limit who can comment on your posts and decide whether strangers can ask for your friendship after subscribing to your feed.

The ticker

You'll have noticed a running scroll in the upper right-hand corner of your screen. Known as the **ticker**, this miniaturized news feed relays events across your Facebook universe as they unfold in real-time. While your regular-sized feed only reports the things you might have some interest in, the ticker throws everything at you, even revealing your friends'

Hovering your mouse over the ticker reveals a sidebar that lets you scroll through all the updates made by your friends – including updates in which your friends are tagged – from the last few hours.

comments and actions on people's pages with whom you have no connection whatsoever.

And it's always with you – you'll find it occupying the same place in your timeline as it does on your home page. Clicking on an entry will bring up a window that displays the entire post. From there, you can comment, like or share, just as if the post were in your regular news feed.

TIP: You can shrink or stretch the ticker by pulling on the tab between it and the chat box below.

Chatting

Instant messaging has been both a wonder and a drain to productivity, giving people the chance to find solutions quickly in a global workplace, but also enabling nonstop chatter. Distraction aside, it's great for communicating with people overseas or when a phone call might prove

49

Video chat

Video chat is becoming as common as a phone call, and thanks to services like Skype and **Google Chat** (see p.235) it won't cost you anything more than what you already pay for high-speed Internet service. Facebook has joined with Skype so that you can talk to your friends face-to-face (so to speak) – all you need is a microphone and a camera, plus a little bit of software that Facebook provides automatically, and it'll be like you're in the same room. Just open a regular chat window and click the video icon; Facebook will do

the rest. You can even leave a video message for friends who aren't currently online.

disruptive, and since it's not as formal as an email you can get away with shorthand (see p.140).

It's all very straightforward. Simply click a friend in your **chat window**, and start typing. Even if they aren't currently online or available to chat, you can still write to them and they'll receive your IM the next time they log in. Chat will remember your entire correspondence,

When you receive a message or friend request, or if someone comments on one of your photos or status updates, you'll see an alert at the top of your Facebook screen.

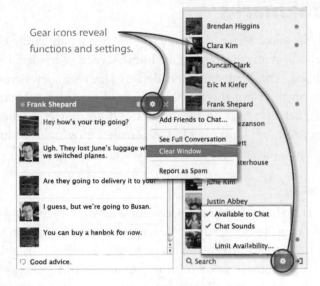

Gear icons reveal functions and settings.

Green lights in your chat list tell you which of your friends are online.

even if you close the window, and will save the entire thread in your **messages** (see overleaf).

While you're chatting with one friend, you can add another to the same exchange to create a **group chat.** And if you ever become tired of the audio alert that chimes every time you get a new message, or if you want to take yourself offline altogether, click on the gear icon at the base of the chat window and select the appropriate option. While there, you can also limit your chat availability using lists (see p.59).

51

Bookmarks

To help make sense of the flurry of activity happening on Facebook at any given time, the **home** screen is divided into columns. The centre column defaults to your news feed. Over on the right there's space reserved for the ticker and your chat list. And on the left is the **bookmarks sidebar**. Organized by kind, bookmarks make moving through Facebook quicker and easier than searching.

Messages

You'll find links to your news feed, messages and events under your favourite bookmarks. **Messages** are a combination of saved chats and private emails with your Facebook friends. Clicking the message icon brings you to your inbox, where you can engage with all of your current conversations or start a new message thread with one of your friends. You'll have to open a conversation and use the actions menu to **delete** or **forward** it, **add people** to or **leave** a group conversation, or you can hide it by choosing **archive** – an archived message will disappear from your inbox and will only reappear if your friend writes back (you can also find archived messages using **search messages**, found at the top of your message box).

TIP: Claim your @facebook email address by following the prompts at the very top of your messages page. Now people can write to you at your Facebook account from any email service.

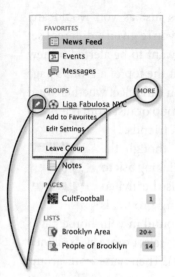

Hover your mouse over any **bookmark** to reveal an edit icon. Hovering also brings up the **more** option, which shows a list of all bookmarks not currently in the sidebar.

Events

The other mainstay of the sidebar, **events**, keeps track of your social calendar while letting you peek in on your friends' upcoming public engagements. Click the calendar bookmark to create a **new event** at a time and place of your choosing, then invite your friends. Here, you can also accept event **invitations** from friends, add comments about a gathering, and invite more people to someone else's event if the organizer has allowed the option. Events also let you know when a friend's **birthday** is approaching, and will send an alert to your news feed so you don't forget.

Groups

Groups are collections of people brought together under a common interest – find them using the search bar at the top of the Facebook page. You don't have to be friends with the individual members of a group, though it's a good place to meet people who like the same things as you.

You'll interact with group pages just as you would any individual's page on Facebook, but you're given a different set of options for how and when you want to be alerted to new posts. Click the **notifications** box at the top of a group's page and choose **settings**. From here, you can select whether you'd like to hear from everyone in the group or just from members who are also your regular Facebook friends.

Groups are closed to outsiders, though the application process is as simple as clicking **ask to join group** on their page. You may also be invited by a member of the group. Creating groups is just as easy. Click **create a group**, found in your home page's bookmarks (if you don't see it listed, select **more** as explained in the caption on the previous page). Then name your group, select an icon and invite your first potential members. You can also set the privacy level, including the impossibile-to-find-unless-you're-invited **secret group** option.

Apps

Apps, short for applications, are programs that run inside Facebook. They can be practical or nonsensical, save you time, promote your business (see p.98) or help fritter away the last few hours of work before the weekend.

> **TIP:** If you don't see the app you're looking for in your bookmarks, and can't find it after clicking the **more** button, check under **account settings** for a complete and fully editable list (see p.90).

When you click on an approved application, you're taken to a new screen with the app prominently displayed and an **application ticker** in place of the news feed ticker. Every app is different, but the app ticker will always show who among your friends is currently using an app. You can comment on your friends' app activity through the ticker, or click through to the app they're using and add it to your own list.

Many apps, especially games, will entice you with a free version, only to suggest that you might advance more quickly if only you purchased some add-ons. While credit cards and PayPal are happily accepted, **Facebook Credit** (see p.97) is the preferred currency – rather than buy from individual apps, you can buy tokens directly from Facebook and use them to fund your purchases within apps. You can even buy gift cards full of credits at Tesco and Walmart.

Along the top of the app ticker are icons representing recently used apps, and a drop-down navigation panel that also tells you your current Facebook credit balance.

Get appy!

With all the services and features within Facebook, you'd think there'd be no room for more. Oh, how far that is from the truth! App developers have taken to using Facebook as a platform to run their own programs, and more than twenty million apps are installed into Facebook accounts every day. To get you started, we've suggested some of the best and most popular apps – you can find them by entering their names into the search bar at the top of your Facebook screen. If you'd like to uncover more, try using www.appfishing.com (which just so happens to be a Facebook app for finding Facebook apps).

Learn and explore

The best apps take an experience you enjoy outside of Facebook, and redesign it so it works as part of the site. News services such as the **Guardian** and **Wall Street Journal** have created apps that let you read their articles and share them with your friends as naturally as if you were interacting with any page in Facebook. Airlines have begun integrating full service features into their apps, with **Delta Ticket Counter** and **Flying Social with Alaska Airlines** leading the way (the latter will find your friends on a map of North America, and include the price of a ticket to their location). Listen to music with **Spotify**, share your reading list with **Virtual Bookshelf**, stream television with **Hulu** – continue to explore and you'll be amazed by what you find.

Social games

Facebook's apps may be wide-ranging, but games are its biggest draw. Long standing atop the popularity pile are a series of 'ville games (**FarmVille**, **CityVille**, **FrontierVille**), which use a levelling-up system to encourage players to return again and again. Beloved classics like **Tetris Battle** and **Scrabble** have been updated to include social connectivity letting you play with friends online and compare your results on network scoreboards. If you're looking for a fun distraction, you may enjoy the following:

▶ **Hanging with Friends:** A lot like "hangman" but with the added element of Scrabble-style point accumulation.

▶ **Biotronic:** This pattern-matching challenge is a more elaborate Bejeweled (which is also available as an app).

▶ **CivWorld:** The Facebook version of Sid Meyer's groundbreaking Civilization, where the world is yours to create.

▶ **Texas HoldEm Poker:** The game that made poker a televised sport – you can take it with you if you're on a streak (see p.82).

▶ **Pixel Ranger:** You're a low-res cowboy with a shotgun, protecting your land from equally low-res creatures.

▶ **Gunshine:** Band together with friends in search of fame and fortune in this massively multiplayer role-playing game.

▶ **Sim Social:** A life-simulation game from the genre's originators (first developed in the year 2000).

Pages

Facebook encourages organizations, businesses and causes to create a **page** as their landing pad within the site rather than signing up as if they were a person. Instead of friends, pages receive likes, and while individuals are limited to five thousand friends, there is no limit to the number of likes a page can receive. If you have a business of your own and have set up a page for it (see p.98), you will find a link to it here, within your bookmarks. Otherwise, you won't see pages as an option among your bookmarks.

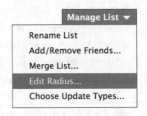

Location-based lists let you choose how near your friends must be for inclusion.

Facebook notes

While status updates and comments tend to be more off-the-cuff affairs, the **notes application** (if not already in your bookmarks sidebar, search for "notes" using the search box at the top of the page) encourages you to take your time and get your wording, spelling and formatting just right. Using a style toolbar akin to those in fully fledged word processing programs, you can adjust your text to look exactly the way you'd like, save it as a draft if you haven't the time to finish it at the moment, and post it when it's in a shape you're happy to share with your friends.

Selecting **show all lists** also gives you the option of creating a brand-new list. Just be careful you don't slip and hit **unfriend** along the way.

Lists

One of the best ways to organize your many friends is to sort them using lists. You can make as many lists as you like and put as many of your friends within them as you want – though it helps to stick people together who share some common trait. Then, you can use your lists to share updates or converse with specific groups of people rather than everyone at once. Simply navigate to a friend's timeline and hover your mouse over the **friends** option. From there you can add or remove her from one or more lists.

Facebook also creates a number of **smart lists** based on the information you provide about your hometown and your schooling. You may want to add or remove people from these lists, or edit a list's properties to automatically include more or less people. Head to your **home** page and click the link to that list in the left sidebar (if you don't see it, select **more** at the bottom of the sidebar, and also **more** next to lists). Then click **manage list** to reveal options for organizing its members.

Timeline

The **timeline** represents the totality of your Facebook persona. Stretching back to the day you were born, the timeline organizes by date every event you've recorded on Facebook to this very instant. You can move up and down the timeline, filling in gaps and expanding on previous posts, or highlighting significant events so they stand out for visitors to your page. It's also where you manage your friends, likes, photos and notes.

Now
September
August
July
2012
2011
2010
2009
2008
2007
2006
2005
2000
1993
Born

Chose your cover

First impressions being generally regarded as influential, you'll want to spend a little time sorting out just the right image for your timeline's **cover pic**. The cover sits behind your profile picture (see p.32), providing a splash of colour reminiscent of the header area on a website. Hovering your mouse over your cover pic will bring up a box that lets you **adjust positioning**, or choose a whole new photo if you become bored with your current selection. Cover pics are much wider than they are tall, so it's best to choose an image with a horizontal, or landscape, orientation. If you find that your favourite photo doesn't quite work, it may still be possible to edit it to fit (see p.69).

Add a Cover ▼

Explore your history

It's easy enough to scroll through your posts, but depending on how long you've been active there might be quite a bit to sift through. To relieve your mouse of some of its burden, Facebook shortens the timeline by hiding older posts. Clicking a date range along the line will reveal all the hidden activity within that period.

> **TIP:** Hold your mouse over the timeline until a plus sign appears, and you'll be able to insert a post retroactively.

You might also want to know how often you've used an application, or when it was that you first heard that song that's now stuck in your head. Rather than wandering through your timeline looking for clues, click the **view activity** button and select the appropriate application from the drop-down list (initially marked **all**), or unfold a group of your favourite applications hidden below your friends and photos bookmarks (see overleaf).

Updating events

Just like when you're on your home page browsing the news feed, you're able to update your status and

Facebook tracks your every move and takes note any time you're mentioned, then displays the highlights at the top of your timeline.

add pictures and videos to your timeline (see p.71). Here, though, you're also able to highlight **life events** – important happenings that stand out from your regular routine. Bought a puppy? Earned a promotion? Click an event icon in your status bar, select the appropriate subject and fill in the blanks. Life events are much more visible on your timeline than any normal status, so make them count!

Use @**name** when you reference a friend in one of your status posts. You'll be given a

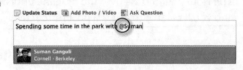

drop-down menu of possibilities and your chosen friend will be sent a message letting them know they've made your timeline.

Timeline bookmarks

Although the timeline is arranged in an entirely different fashion to your news feed, some of the same features are available on both pages – they just look, and sometimes act, differently. Case in point are **bookmarks**. We've seen how bookmarks make it easy to jump from your news feed to different areas of the site (see p.52), and in your timeline they behave in a similar fashion (although here they're entirely limited to applications). Want to see a list of your friends, or manage your photos (see p.65)? What about editing your favourites and **likes** (see

The timeline has its own bookmarks that you can rearrange as you see fit. Click the arrow to expand the panel and reveal your whole list.

p.37), or adjusting your **subscriptions**? The answers can be found behind a timeline bookmark.

You can't delete your friends or photos bookmarks, but the rest are only there because you allow them to be. Hover your mouse over any other bookmark and the tiny edit icon will appear. Click it and you'll be able to change, move or delete that bookmark. Use your slots wisely – you only get twelve timeline bookmarks, and you'll start out with half that amount by default. To fill in the blanks, just click the **plus symbol** in the empty slot and you'll be shown a list of possible additions.

> **TIP:** Click the gear icon above your timeline bookmarks, then select **view as...** to see what your timeline looks like to other people – especially useful after making adjustments to your privacy settings (see p.74).

Locations

Any time you update your status or upload a photo or video, you're encouraged to provide a location. It's a nice way of remembering where you've been, but clicking on each photo or update to check on your travels seems like

When you record your location on a photo, status update or in your profile information, you'll leave a mark on your map of the world.

a lot of work. Thanks to the **map** app, you'll see an immediate visual representation of your peregrinations.

Whenever you include a **location** on a photo or life event, a pin is automatically dropped on your map. As pins accumulate in one spot they transform into larger and larger circles, within which is a number representing how frequently you visit the same places. Zooming in on a specific area of the map – either by using the plus and minus controls, or by clicking on a map point – will dissolve the circles, turning them back into separate points. Selecting a point will bring you directly to the event or photo, letting you edit or adjust it as you see fit.

TIP: You can refine location searches by **story** type, as indicated along the bottom of your map. Choosing a story type limits the number of pins on your map to just those instances.

Photos

Facebook isn't just about sharing your thoughts, it's also about sharing your experiences – and what better way to share what you've seen than to post a photo of it? Photos are a great way to liven up your timeline, and they help keep distant friends up to date with your travel adventures, special events and celebrations. You might also just come across something poignant or humorous and want to let your friends know about it. Whatever the case, Facebook has ways to help you organize and share photos with some or all of your friends, or with the public at large.

Sharing

There are a few ways to send photos from your computer to Facebook The first is by adding a photo as part of a **status update** – by way of either your timeline or your home page – for which the photo will be automatically added to your wall photo album (see overleaf). You can also take a picture with your **webcam** and post the

Hover your mouse over photos and videos in your timeline to reveal quick editing and display options.

result to your status immediately, or
start a new album and post the cover
picture as part of your status.

+ Add Photos

Organizing

Rather than uploading photos in piecemeal fashion, you're
encouraged to organize them into **albums**. Albums offer
some broad **privacy** features, and have the advantage of
providing a sense of order to what might otherwise become
a junk drawer full of snapshots. You gain access to your
albums via your timeline – click the **photos** bookmark and
you'll be presented with all of your current albums, along
with the option of creating new ones.

Initially, you'll have at least one album that's been
created by Facebook to hold all of your **profile pictures**.
You cannot delete this album (though you can remove
individual photos at any time), and any photo you select
for your profile pic will automatically find its way here. To
edit or remove a photo from this album, simply click that
photo and choose the appropriate selection from the list of
options displayed.

> **TIP:** Popular photo services **Flickr** and **Picasa** will let you share
> images and albums to your Facebook account – though neither
> works quite the same way. Flickr requires a settings adjustment
> in your account (see p.90), while Picasa will get you to download
> a stand-alone application called the Picasa Uploader.

Editing albums

When you **add photos** to the photo page, Facebook will prompt you to create a new album. While the files upload in the background, you'll be asked to name and describe the album. You're also given the option of using standard or high-resolution files (the standard option is more than adequate for viewing on a computer screen) as well as the chance to choose a privacy selection.

You can create as many albums as you'd like, and set privacy options on a case-by-case basis. If you're dissatisfied with the order in which they're displayed, click and drag them into whatever arrangement you'd prefer.

Once you have an album in place, you can add or remove photos from it, update descriptive and location information for the album or the individual photos within, rearrange the order of the images, change the album cover and **tag your friends** in group shots. To uncover these options, first click the album you want to edit, then look for the

Photo tips

Facebook is a little like a scrapbook – it's a place where we record events in words and pictures to remember and share with our friends. For the written portion you'll have to rely on your years spent studying the language, but for pics there are loads of editing programs, plus some easy-to-follow tips, that can help give your images a touch of style.

Taking proper photos

You can't change an orange into a banana, and you won't be able to edit a terrible photo to make it great. Following a few simple guidelines when lining up your shots will give your photographs a little more zing.

▶ **Turn off the flash** Don't let your camera wash away all subtlety with its auto-flash. You can capture much more nuance in dim natural lighting with a longer exposure time.

▶ **The rule of thirds** It's tempting to sit the subject of your photo smack in the middle of the shot. But a more interesting composition might appear when you divide the shot into thirds and position key elements where the divisions intersect.

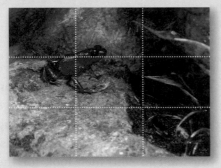

▶ **Get up close** Capturing a far-off monument with a speck of a person deep in the frame is an all-too-common occurrence. Bring people to the foreground, and let backgrounds stay in the background.

▶ **Change the orientation** A camera is designed to be held horizontally, but that shouldn't stop you from flipping it on its end. People in particular tend to look more like they do in real life when you capture them lengthways.

Adjusting your images

Sometimes the "perfect pic" isn't quite as perfect as you thought it was. Fortunately, there are numerous photo editing programs available online, many of which are free to use. Rotating, cropping, resizing, adjusting lighting, taking out red-eye are all standard fare in the options listed below. These programs also integrate seamlessly with Facebook, as well as with online photo management sites such as **Flickr** and **Picasa** (see p.238).

▶ **Pixenate** http://pixenate.com

▶ **Fotoflexer** http://fotoflexer.com

▶ **Picknik** www.picknik.com

▶ **Phixr** www.phixr.com

edit album selection above the photos. Here you'll be able to make changes at the album level, but to adjust its contents you'll have to go further. Continue on by clicking the **edit photos** option in the lower left of the box – now you can adjust descriptions for individual photos, reorder them, or remove them entirely.

Tagging

Facebook can sense when you add a photo of a person or a group of people to one

When editing photos within an album, you can choose to make any photo the album cover and move photos between albums using the drop-down menu.

of your albums, and will ask you to tell it the names of those people in a process called **tagging**. If you're already friends with a person that you're tagging, they'll be alerted by Facebook message. And you don't have to tag the photo as you're uploading it to an album – clicking on any photo in your news feed or timeline, regardless of whether you're the owner of the photo, will expand the image so it fills your screen, and from there you can click **tag**, select the person you know and save the update by selecting **done tagging**.

Video

Though YouTube is the firm favourite for sharing amateur videos (see p.262), Facebook also allows you to upload and save videos alongside your photo albums, and even to record messages to your timeline using a **webcam**.

Editing video

You'll need to make sure your videos aren't more than twenty minutes long and have a file size no larger than one gigabyte.

+ Add Videos

Unfortunately, Facebook doesn't provide anything in the way of video editing, so you'll have to go to outside sources for that.

Mac owners can use **iMovie** to edit video right on their desktop, while PC users might want to try the most recent Windows version of **Movie Maker**. These programs include audio and video tools that can crop, rearrange, overlay effects and create titles – if you have the patience to experiment with all the features. There are also more limited, but often easier-to-use video editors that work entirely online – meaning you won't have to install any new software on your computer. Just sign up for one of the services below, upload the video you want to edit and add the result to your Facebook page.

▶ **Pixorial** www.pixorial.com

▶ **Creaza** www.creazaeducation.com/movieeditor

▶ **Movie Masher** www.moviemasher.com

Unlike with photos, where clicking on a picture in your timeline or news feed expands the image and presents some immediate editing features, clicking on a video will just play the video. If you want to make any adjustments to the video's **description** or tag the people in it, you'll need to find your way to where it's saved. From your timeline click **photos**, then look for the small blue **videos** link next to **your albums**. From here you can make adjustments to individual videos or delete them altogether.

✓ On your timeline · Remove

Title: **Explosive Bora!**
Share with: 👥 **Friends** ▾

Tag This Video
Edit This Video
Delete Video
Embed this Video

◈ ◈

Facebook's video editing options are minimal, but you can flip the perspective horizontally or vertically, and find a link that will let you **embed** your video in a blog or other outside website.

After watching a video through to its end, you're given the option of sending it by message or sharing it to a friend's timeline. You can also post it to the news feed for any group of which you're a part. Select **share** to open a new window where you can include your friends' names and set the privacy level (to save potential embarrassment).

The movie player is set up to handle widescreen footage, but won't balk at standard proportions.

Commenting with photos and video

Posting content to your own timeline only makes up a portion of the Facebook experience – you'll inevitably want to comment on what your friends are doing as well (see p.46). That includes sharing photos and videos directly on their timelines, rather than exclusively on your own.

When adding a fresh comment to a friend's page, the same options will be available as when you're about to make an update to yours – including the choice of uploading a photo or video. You can use any item already saved to your albums, upload a new file from your computer or capture a photo or video right there using a webcam. **Video uploads** are not immediately obvious – they're hidden behind the prompt to upload a photo.

You're also able to share pictures and videos you find from YouTube and other places around the web. For this to work, simply **copy the link** to the video or picture directly into the post portion of the update box (avoiding the suggestion to upload a photo). Facebook will think for a bit before a thumbnail image of your video or photo appears. From there, you can add a comment about the link you've shared or adjust the automatically included description by hovering your mouse over it until it lights up, then clicking on it once to make the text editable.

Privacy

After sending off your first round of invitations, you should soon start seeing friends show up in your news feed. Just as you can see what they've been up to, these people will be able to read everything you've posted and see every photo and video in which you've been tagged. While you might not have a problem with some of your friends knowing every little detail of your life, there are probably a few whom you'd rather keep more in the dark.

Covering your tracks

Previous sections have pointed out some case-by-case privacy options and suggested how you might use **lists** to help limit who can see your individual posts (see p.59). For better overall control, click on the little arrow in the upper right corner of your Facebook screen, and select **privacy settings**. You'll see a reminder of how to adjust privacy on individual posts and a suggestion to set your **default privacy**. Choosing the right default setting will save you the hassle of selecting more or less privacy for your posts en masse.

Facebook maintains a consistent look for its privacy icons across the entire site. Know them once, know them always.

Next on the list is the option of **limiting your connections**. These choices represent a first line of defence against strangers filling your **message box** with requests, and can stop friends muddying your timeline with nonsense posts. You can also throw a wall up around your timeline so that only selected friends can see what other people post about you.

> **TIP:** Custom privacy settings give you the option of hiding posts from specific individuals or particular lists of friends.

Cut off the tags

Default settings and privacy drop-down menus are all well and good, but those solutions are for when you originate a status update or post a photo to your own timeline. All bets are off when you're named in a friend's photo or mentioned in one of their posts. Fear not, there are still ways to limit your exposure.

While still on your privacy screen, choose to edit the settings for **how tags work**. Normally, when you're mentioned in a post or marked present in a photo or video, an indication is sent to your timeline for all your friends to see. This might result in your revealing an activity you'd rather have kept quiet. To stop sharing so freely and give yourself a chance to look over what it is

Whenever you're tagged with review enabled, you'll receive an alert next to the **view activity** button on your timeline.

you're being accused of, enable both **timeline review** and **tag review**. The former will hold any outside addition to your timeline in a queue until you give it the OK, while the latter lets you approve or reject tags to photos and videos in which you've been identified.

Even if you've agreed to allow anyone to tag you in photos or to post to your timeline, you can still limit who sees these tags using the **maximum timeline visibility** option. Operating as a final filter, changing the visibility can stop any automatically approved additions to your timeline from being seen by the general public. Using options similar to the default privacy settings, you're even able to limit who can see updates that made it through your timeline and tag reviews.

> **TIP:** Hide your timeline from strangers by disabling **public search**, found on the apps and websites privacy settings page.

To help deflect a potential torrent of tags, you might further discourage tagging by adjusting the **tag suggestions**

You are blocked! ⊖

There's a particular school of thought that considers hell to be other people, and after some time on Facebook you may find yourself in agreement. Knowing how annoying it can be to deal with unwanted advances, Facebook has come up with a number of ways to hide your account from undesirables. To get started, head to your privacy page (see p.74), then select **manage blocking**.

The first level of privacy on offer is the option of restricting a friend's ability to see anything but your public posts. Your friend won't be sent an alert about the change, so unless they pay particular attention to the privacy levels in their news feed, they'll be none the wiser.

Blocking a person outright is a stronger, but sometimes necessary, course of action. You can **block** someone even if they've never been your friend, and from then on you won't see them, and they can't see you. Blocking a person also makes it impossible for them to search for you through Facebook, though if you belong to the same group (see p.53) they'll still see you in the members list.

You can also block **application** and **event invites** – helpful when you have friends who want you to join them in an unwelcome game, or meet them for a regular get-together of which you'd rather not be a part. Here's where you can also stop the apps you do use from filling your news feed with alerts.

and **places** options. Tag suggestions uses facial recognition software to try to identify your features in pictures, while the places feature lets friends include you as having accompanied them while out and about. Disabling one or both can help cut down on a backlog of timeline and tag activity alerts.

Restricting apps and websites

When you sign up for a Facebook account, you simultaneously give them the right to make your name, gender, networks of friends and profile pic public information. You can limit who can contact you and how much strangers can see using some of the features described above, but when it comes to **apps and websites** it's back to square one.

Privacy settings for your apps can also be accessed through the account settings toolbar (see p.90).

Any app you sign up for will immediately request access to portions of your profile, and unless you agree you won't be able to use the app. Sometimes the request is reasonable. It's understandable why some apps might want to access your basic information and friends list (the better to sell you products or hook you up with friends who are already using the same app), but requirements sometimes involve releasing photos, expanded profile information and even the right to access your information when you're offline. You can limit some of these without giving up your ability to use an app by **editing the privacy settings** for individual apps.

If you have a lot of apps, adjusting settings on an app-by-app basis quickly becomes tedious. You might consider simply deleting the ones you no longer use, and adjusting settings for those that remain. Alternatively, you can **turn off all platform apps**. This, though, is a drastic option, because if you decide you don't want to share any of your information with any app at any time, you are effectively turning off your ability to use any Facebook app.

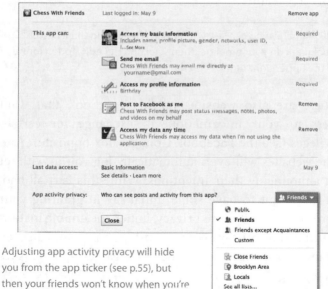

Adjusting app activity privacy will hide you from the app ticker (see p.55), but then your friends won't know when you're available to collaborate.

Considering that companies have seemingly innumerable ways to mine your personal data (just think of all the spam and junk mail you receive every day), you may as well resolve yourself to the fact that they're going to reach you, and focus on the positives – mainly, that you get to use their apps and services for your own personal gratification. But that doesn't mean all your friends need to see when you're checking your horoscope online. **App activity privacy** can only be adjusted on the settings page for each app, so as you determine whether you want to keep an app or delete it, take the time to dip in and toggle its privacy feature.

> **TIP:** Manage who can see your friends by clicking the **friends** bookmark on your timeline, then selecting the **edit** option found in the upper right of the screen.

There are also websites outside Facebook that want access to your information, in exchange for certain privileges (see the Facebook Connect box opposite). And some websites will even automatically log you in without first announcing their intentions. While this isn't all bad, you may want to have some initial say in granting your approval. For a bit more privacy, untick the **enable instant personalization on partner websites** box found behind instant personalization on the apps, games and websites privacy page.

Facebook Connect

As you flit about the web, absorbing your daily share of news, gossip and entertainment, you'll notice the option of signing into certain services using your Facebook account. Known from the development side as **Facebook Connect** (see p.110), this far-reaching feature offers a work around to creating an unique account on every site you visit.

Websites that want you to join them using your Facebook information will ask you to approve an app, then request access to your personal data. If you agree, you'll make some

of that personal information available to them, but they can't sell it or use it outside the scope of their application. They will use it to serve more appropriate ads while you're on their site, though on the plus side they'll also try to send you more appropriate content. Agreeing also makes it easier to share the things you come across with your friends back on Facebook, and often offers the options of commenting on and "liking" stories and services for display in your timeline.

If you happen to find the idea of sharing your password with outside sites a little too insecure, you have the option of creating **unique access codes** that will work for many sites and outside applications which use Facebook Connect. For more on this, and for other ways to strengthen account security, see p.92.

Facebook mobile

With smarter and smarter phones being produced at an accelerating rate, coupled with the ability to transmit data ever more quickly across the airwaves, it seems that just about everything you once did on a desktop computer can now be accomplished right in the palm of your hand. As Facebook is a service that encourages sharing what you've done in as close to real-time as possible, it seems a natural fit to have it working through your mobile phone. With its location-based features and mapping functions, Facebook mobile makes keeping track of where you are, who you're with and what you're doing all the easier.

Mobile web browsers

If you have a phone that's capable of connecting to the web, then you'll be able to access a version of Facebook on the go. How robust a version depends on the sophistication of your phone's web browser. Most Internet-enabled phones will let you see your **news feed** (see p.42), **messages** (see p.52) and **friend requests**. You'll also be able to update your status, comment on what's happening in your friends' worlds and peruse your

For Facebook to work on your mobile phone, you'll need an active Internet connection provided either by mobile data service (as part of your phone plan) or through Wi-Fi.

previously uploaded photos. Point your browser to www.facebook.com and watch as it transforms into m.facebook.com. Then simply use the same login information you'd use for the full version of the site.

> **TIP:** Upload photos, videos and status updates by emailing them to your Facebook page. Go to **www.facebook.com/mobile** and copy the secret email address into your address book. Now you can add breaking news and real-time photos to your timeline from any Internet-enabled phone.

The smartest phones

Android and **iPhone** owners have access to a wide suite of features that, while not as far reaching as the computer-based website, bring the mobile experience quite close to the desktop version. Though uploading a photo or video remains the stuff of apps (see p.86), you can do just about everything else through the mobile website. And with large, vivid touchscreens making for easier navigation and functionality, much of

Icons and their functions (like recent **notifications**) remain consistent across platforms.

what you'll see will look and act in a way that's already familiar to you.

After logging in, you'll be taken directly to your news feed, with top and recent stories displayed in the usual order, and new message alerts and friend requests highlighted along the top. Tiny plus signs accompany each news item, behind which you can **like** or **comment** – strictly written comments, that is. You can also update your own status, or indicate your location using the **check in** button.

Mobile check-in uses a combination of GPS, Wi-Fi hotspots and phone tower locations to approximate your position on the planet. Clicking its icon generates a list of businesses nearby.

Online sidebar

As it does for the desktop version of Facebook (see p.52), the bookmarks sidebar makes quick work of navigation in **smartphone** versions of the mobile site. Tap the triple lined icon in the upper left of your phone's screen to release the sidebar, and from there you'll have access to all your favourites, apps, groups, lists and any **pages** you may

administer (see p.98). Tapping the same icon will slide the sidebar back where it came from, reinstating the full-screen view you'd just covered.

Most of these features work in exactly the same way as their desktop counterparts, with a few notable exceptions.

For one, you can't upload photos, but you can still access your albums and make comments on photos you've previously added by way of the **photo** bookmark. There's also the automatic addition to your favourites of the **nearby** bookmark. Selecting this icon will show you a list of all your friends who have recently updated their locations (the "nearby" designation is a bit of a misnomer, as this list will include anyone on the same continent as you). Here, you'll also be encouraged to update your own location, managed in similar fashion to the main site (see p.64).

You'll also notice that, along with the help centre, a number of settings are on display, whereas on the full version of the site they're secreted away under a drop-down menu (see p.90). Changes you make to the account, privacy and security settings on your mobile will translate back to the main website – including adjustments to your language settings (see p.35).

Mobile apps

Statistics suggest that while mobile web access to Facebook grows by a considerable percentage each year, the number of us using some version of the **Facebook app** on our phones is even greater. Using an app can get around certain mobile web browser restrictions, like **posting photos** to a status or uploading videos to an album from your phone.

Smartphones with connections to an app store, like the Android market and BlackBerry's app world, will find a free version of the Facebook app within. The interface will vary from phone to phone, but not so much that you'll be out of your depth, and touchscreen versions look and act in a similar way to the mobile web version already discussed in the smartphone section (see p.83).

Including a picture as part of a status update starts with selecting the camera icon – an option exclusive to the Facebook mobile app.

For those with web-enabled "dumb" phones, there may still be an app that works, thanks to **Facebook for every phone**. Send your browser to d.facebook.com/install and follow the prompts to save the app onto your phone. Now you can search for friends in your phone contacts, upload photos, check the latest feeds and message your friends more quickly and efficiently than through the clunky web portal.

Outside apps

Even within the Facebook mobile app, you'll have access to the apps you're used to seeing from the desktop version – including any **games** or **services** you're subscribed to. Rather than overwhelm your phone's tiny brain with apps running inside apps, you'll often be prompted to download your games and services separately from Facebook. When you do, you'll log in to them using your regular Facebook credentials, and your usage and results will be saved so that everything stays in sync between your desktop and your phone.

Facebook Messenger

While you can send messages from the Facebook app and the mobile version as well, the stand-alone **messenger app** is significantly easier to use (and much less likely to crash). Available for all smartphones, messenger keeps you logged in at all times so friends can reach you **instantly** even while you're on the go. You can also create group chats that include people from outside Facebook, as selected from your phone's contact list. You're even able to embed photos for comment, and you can turn on alerts so you're pinged whenever you receive a new message.

TIP: If you need to see the desktop layout instead of the mobile website version on your smartphone, navigate to the bottom of the sidebar and choose **desktop site**.

Status control

Our work and home lives tend to inspire quite different sorts of status updates, but it's time spent between the two that can be the most exciting. Instead of waiting until you're sitting back in front of a computer, Facebook mobile allows you to instantly **update your status** from either the news feed or your timeline, with one difference – you can't tweak your status while viewing it in your news feed on the mobile version. Any change you want to make after you post will have to be done from your timeline. But it's easy enough. Simply click on your name in the sidebar, tap the post in question and adjust. And, if by the time you get there someone has made a comment you're not happy about, you can remove it by opening the comments for that post and choosing the delete option – on smartphones that means sliding your finger from right to left over the offending comment, then tapping the delete button that appears. Everything you add, delete or adjust on the mobile version shows up on the desktop version.

Slide your finger from right to left across the add comment symbol in your mobile timeline to reveal the option of **deleting** your own post.

SMS alerts

Even without a web browser on your phone, you can interact with your Facebook account using simple text message commands. First you'll need to attach your phone number to your Facebook account. From your desktop computer, click the tiny arrow in the upper right of the Facebook screen and choose **account settings** (for more on these, see overleaf), then select **mobile** from the options on the left. You'll be asked for your mobile number and then be required to text a code to Facebook in order to start the whole thing going.

Once you've confirmed your number, choose whether you want to share it with your friends and if you'd like them to be able to text your phone from Facebook. Then, on the page that follows, select **notifications** and adjust when Facebook should alert you about comments, requests or security updates. You can change these settings any time you'd like – including restricting the number of texts you receive each day – by returning to the same mobile settings page. As for texting commands to Facebook (the bold term is the command):

▶ Add a new friend: **add** Suman Ganguli

▶ Subscribe to someone's posts: **subscribe** Sean Mahoney

▶ Unsubscribe from someone's: **unsubscribe** Sean Mahoney

▶ Poke a friend: **poke** Frank Shepard

▶ Update your status: **is** waiting for the train.

▶ Stop receiving texts: **stop**

Account settings

There are ways to manage Facebook's behaviour within posts and albums, using lists and subscriptions (see p.47), and through individual and global privacy selections (see p.74). But there's only one place you can alter your very identity on the site, or remove yourself entirely if you so desire: in your account settings.

Click the arrow in the upper right of your Facebook screen, select **account settings** and from there you can finely tune your Facebook experience.

▼
Account Settings
Privacy Settings
Use Facebook as Page
Log Out
Help Center

General adjustments

When you first signed up for Facebook, you included some pretty basic information, including your name, email address and a password to secure your account from devious intent. But names may change by marriage or divorce, emails can transfer due to a new job or service,

and passwords should rotate out with some regularity. All this information can be adjusted in the **general settings**.

Account setting subsections are found on the left of the page, in a list similar to the bookmarks on your home page.

Here, too, is where you can change your Facebook username, select a new primary network (in the event you change jobs or schools) and enter a **nickname** that will display next to your proper name on your timeline. You can also link certain other online accounts – like Google and Yahoo! – to Facebook, so when you log in to those accounts you'll simultaneously log in to Facebook. This  linking is performed through a service called **OpenID** and is intended to create a more seamless online experience while also providing an added layer of security.

How might logging in to different sites without actually logging in to them be more secure? Well, the theory suggests that without having so many different log in procedures and **security** prompts popping up every time you need to use one of your services, you'll be less likely to unwillingly feed your information to a hacker. And OpenID is not owned by any one service – not by Facebook or Google or LinkedIn – meaning that your identity is technically controlled exclusively by you.

> **TIP:** If you want to keep a copy of all your Facebook photos, videos, status updates, messages, chats and contacts on your own computer, request an archive of it all by clicking on **download a copy** in the general settings page. You'll receive an email with a download link when it's ready.

Security

Privacy within Facebook is one thing (see p.74), but unwittingly allowing a hacker or some other malicious entity access to your account is quite another. The first step towards firming up protection against ne'er-do-wells is enabling the **secure browsing** feature.

There will be the subtlest visual difference in the way web addresses look (http:// will become https://), but with the change you'll have added a powerful layer of invisible encryption to your Facebook sessions.

If you'd like to take a more active role in security measures, choose to enable your **login notifications**. These will alert you either by email or text message (see p.95) when someone, including yourself, logs into your account from any computer or mobile phone Facebook doesn't recognize. Combining login notifications with **login approvals** makes for an even more secure account – with approvals turned on, anytime you try to log in to your account from a new machine, Facebook will send a security code to your mobile phone which you'll have to enter through that new machine. The latter service is similar to the verification process you will have stepped through when confirming your mobile phone number as part of your Facebook account (see p.89). After they're approved, you can manage which computers and phones have access to your account using the options inside **recognized devices**.

Deactivate or delete?

No one said you have to stay on Facebook forever, and at some point along the way you may find yourself overwhelmed by just how connected you've become. If events come to pass that encourage you to step away, you have two options – either **deactivate** your account using the option at the bottom of the security page, or **delete** it outright.

Deactivating your account leaves your information intact, but hides it all, so no one (including yourself) can see it. It makes you impossible to find by search, and also removes any comments and tagged photos from your friends pages. As part of the deactivation process you'll be asked your reasons behind the move, and if you manage a group (see p.53), a page or any applications (see p.54) Facebook will ask if you want to remove them too. To reactivate your account, just log back in using your regular info, and everything will be as you left it.

If you're well and truly done with Facebook, first download an archive of your account (see p.91), then fill out the form behind this link: www.facebook.com/help/contact. php?show_form=delete_account. Remember, once you delete your account, there's no turning back.

Clara will miss you

Send Clara a Message

Facebook's deactivation guilt trip includes showing you a selection of friends' photos in which you've been tagged.

To lock down easy access to third-party services that use Facebook Connect (see p.81), it's possible to enable **app passwords**. You may want the benefits of Facebook Connect in place, but instead of sharing your Facebook account information, app passwords gives you a unique access code for logging in. While this may gum up the works on occasion (as not all Facebook Connect-enabled sites agree to this arrangement), it's very helpful if you've also turned on login approvals. Since new machines require activation when login approvals is enabled, you'll have to verify any new machine before using Facebook Connect, even if you're not actually logging in to Facebook on the unregistered device – but using an app password will bypass the normal Facebook machine verification process, and let you start using the outside app right away.

Edit

TIP: Death need not silence Facebook. Memorialize an account for a deceased loved one and it will be held in stasis, able to receive posts in remembrance, but remain otherwise uneditable: www.facebook.com/help/contact.php?show_form=deceased

Perhaps you forget to log out from a **public computer**, or you suspect someone is accessing your account without your knowledge? Check under **active sessions** for a list of all the devices currently logged in to your account. If anything looks suspicious, select **end activity** and your account will be disconnected from that particular device.

Notifications

We've seen how new comments and tags on your posts and photos create an alert at the top of your Facebook page (see p.50) – use **notification settings** to determine which activities are worth such attention. Any activity that lights up your notification icon will also be sent your way by email, though that can quickly fill up your inbox. To combat this, choose to have

one big email roundup sent each week by ticking the **email frequency** box. Other than that, you have the option of fine tuning alerts for all of Facebook's features individually. Tired of seeing your notifications icon light up every time someone likes your post? Want to make sure you receive an email whenever an event is updated? Simply select the feature or app from the list, and choose the options you deem appropriate. Alert options change between every app and feature, but if it's possible to silence, or include, a notification, you will find it here.

> **TIP:** Select the email address where you'd like to receive your notifications in the email field of your general settings (see p.90).

Advertisements

Facebook is free because advertising pays their bills. As long as it remains free, you will not be able to turn off the ads on your page (you may have noticed that as you readjust the width of your browser's screen, the ads will always try to find a way into the frame), but you can at least restrict the use of your name in support of ads shown on your friends' pages. Upon opening the **Facebook Ads** selection in your account settings, you're presented with the options of **editing third party ad settings** and **editing social ad settings**. The former comes into play when a friend logs into an outside website using Facebook Connect (see p.81), while the latter controls whether ads can list you as a supporter within the Facebook website itself.

Seeing as you'd probably endorse those things you've taken the time to "like", it's not entirely disingenuous of advertisers to use your approval while hawking their wares. Still, their gain won't be shared with you, and you're well within your rights to withhold your help. To shut it all off, click each of the aforementioned settings, and within both choose **no one** from the drop-down menus. The change will be invisible to you, but henceforth your friends will not see your name associated with any products on Facebook or anywhere else on the web that Facebook displays ads.

Rough Guides

Browse and buy travel guides and online travel information for world destinations.

👍 Like · Sean Mahoney likes this.

With social ads turned on, friends will see a personal endorsement – which may include your profile picture – in adverts sponsored by business and organizations you "like".

Payments

Facebook may be free to use, but certain apps and services (like Facebook Ads, see p.103) will charge you a fee. Some of the most popular apps use the **freemium** model, where the app itself costs nothing, but enhancements do. In these cases, you might pay the app directly using a credit card or a PayPal account, though if you'd rather not share that information with an app developer, you can purchase **Facebook Credits** to stand for cash (see p.55).

> **TIP:** If you have a **Facebook ads** account, you are required to maintain at least one credit card or PayPal account as your primary funding source. You can only remove the ads funding source on the **ads manager** page (see p.106).

Purchasing credits still requires a credit card or PayPal account, though you can also charge credits to your mobile phone plan, redeem them from a gift card or earn free credits by participating in sponsored activities, like completing surveys or signing up for an insurance quote. Buy or earn credits using the **credits balance** option on the payments page, and check how often you've splurged inside the **credits purchase history** selection. If you'd like to swap out or add an additional credit card, or update its information at any time, you'll find those choices behind **payment methods**.

Facebook for business

With its layers of connectivity and a system that encourages members to share opinions about the products and brands they like best, Facebook is a marketer's dream – but how do you turn that dream into cold hard cash? Online marketing is at best an inexact science, but there are some general rules that anyone with a small (or large) business should follow. Let's step through the process of creating a Facebook presence for your company, then discuss the ways you might best promote your brand and products.

Fan pages

As a business looking to use social media to expand your reach, you'll need to first define a place where potential customers can learn more about your products and services. Sometimes referred to as a landing page in webspeak, this entry portal is called a **fan page** on Facebook. When you first signed up for Facebook, you may have noticed that just below the big green "sign up" button, there was a prompt to create a page. You can reach that page-making option any time by signing out of your personal account – Facebook

Pages aren't limited to businesses, organizations and products. Use them for any cause, will then automatically take you back to that original sign in screen. Alternatively, you'll find a link to **create a page** at the very foot of both your home page (see p.42) and your timeline (see p.60). Or you could point your browser directly to this address: www.facebook.com/pages/create.php.

> **TIP:** Select between your personal and page accounts by clicking the downward arrow in the upper corner of the Facebook screen, and choosing either **use Facebook as page** or **switch back**.

Upon entering page setup, you're presented with various options that will help Facebook get a better handle on what sort of business you are (or type of product you're promoting), then you're prompted by a drop-down menu to further categorize your offerings. The rest is very similar to creating a personal account (see p.28). You're encouraged to post a page **profile photo**, invite current friends and contacts to check out your new page, post an announcement about the whole thing to your personal timeline and to like the page.

Page likes are a very basic form of **analytics**, known on Facebook as **insights** – ways to determine how popular you are among particular demographics (see p.104). They also serve as a mailing list of sorts. As people like your

artistic endeavour or public enterprise that exists outside the bounds of your personal account.

Artist, Band or Public Figure

Entertainment

Cause or Community

page, they're simultaneously agreeing to receive your updates in their news feeds, and if you decide to create an ad (see p.103), they'll be listed as supporters when the ad displays on their friends' pages.

Insights Summary   See All

333 ⇪ Monthly Active Users
  0   New Likes
493 ⇪ News Feed Impressions
  6   Likes and Comments
Insights are visible to page admins only.

Click **see all** in the insights summary box on your page's home screen to reveal data explaining who is visiting your page, and when (see p.104).

Page settings

As with your personal Facebook account, you're able to adjust the way your page behaves by tweaking its settings. While logged in to your page, click its name in the upper corner of the screen to bring up the **wall**. Once there, select the **edit page** button and you'll be taken to a set of options

✏ Edit Page

that let you **manage permissions**. These permissions let you turn your page from public to private, restrict who can see the page by country and age group, set a filter for profanity and restrict certain terms outright. You'll also be able to determine if you'd like your wall, photos or info to be the first page visitors see when they arrive, and what manner of content your fans can post to your page's wall. Here, as well, is where you're given the choice of **deleting your page**, though the deletion process takes two weeks, after which you'll be asked to confirm that you really do want to wipe your page off the rolls.

Profile and administration

You filled in some very limited information about your page during set up, but to better inform fans and visitors about your business you would do well to complete the fields in your **basic information**. Still within edit page, click the option for basic information and you'll be asked to provide an address, contact information and a full description of your business and its products. You can adjust the category of your page, link it to a community of similar services and request a **username** (which results in a shortened web address along the lines of www.facebook.com /yourpage). Establishing a username is particularly useful, as it provides a direct, memorable link to your Facebook page for use in emails, flyers and comment sections around the web.

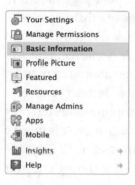

The sidebar on the left of your **edit page** screen will help you navigate between the options.

You'll notice the sidebar includes the option of adjusting your **profile picture** – the process is exactly the same as for your personal account (see p.32) – and you're also able to choose who you'd like to be a **page administrator**. Select **manage admins**, then add the email addresses of anyone you'd like to have full control over your page. Adding someone as an admin allows them to write posts and comments, upload photos and like other pages (see p.37), all in your page's name. They'll also have the ability to change any of your page settings, so choose your admins wisely!

Creating connections

Owning a page isn't just about accepting visitors. It also allows you to wander around Facebook **liking other pages** and commenting on their updates using your page's name. This may seem inconsequential, but it serves a twofold purpose: 1. It encourages other page owners to like your page in return, and 2. It makes you more visible to fans of other pages, who may follow you back to your page, check out your wall and give you a like. **Genuine interaction** is preferred, and will do more good in the long run, so don't go around spamming pages with "check me out" comments. Instead, engage a thread seriously, provide advice where appropriate and only directly encourage people to visit your page if there is specific information relevant to the current conversation. If someone agrees with what you're saying, they'll click through to your page regardless of whether you ask.

> **TIP:** Comments and posts you make on your own page will, by default, be attributed to your page rather than to your personal account – even if you aren't logged in to your page. If you'd like the option of commenting or posting as yourself, head to **your settings** found under edit info (see p.100), and untick the option that reads, "always comment and post on your page as your page, even when using Facebook as your personal account".

Once you've liked a few dozen pages, you can select your favourites and choose to permanently display them in the sidebar on your own page. In the **edit page** settings, choose **featured**, and then click on **edit featured likes**. You'll be able to choose as many pages as you want, but only five will display at any one time, with the rest rotating in with each new visit. While here, you might consider adding yourself and any other admins as **featured page owners**. The selected will be shown in the same sidebar as your featured likes, adding a touch of personality to what might otherwise seem a faceless business.

Cross-promotion and personality are key elements in creating a successful business page.

Advertising

Creating an ad to drive visitors to your page is actually a very simple process in Facebook. Even more encouraging is that ads won't cost you much money for a respectable return – if you use them properly. To get started, click the name of your page in the upper right of the screen so that you're taken to your wall, then choose **promote with an ad** from the shortcuts on the right. You'll be asked to log out of your page (it's okay – Facebook wants a person with a payment

Marketing with insights

We've seen how much data Facebook collects from its 750 million users – everything from gender and location to favourite movies and sports teams. Big companies use this data to focus their ad campaigns on specific groups of people, but they're not the only ones capable of using this information to sell products. All this data can be used by you too. You only need a minimal amount of cash, a bit of patience and the willingness to run through a few phases of trial and error to find out what works, and what doesn't.

When **creating an ad** (see p.103) you'll be required to select a range of people who should receive it. At first you might try limiting your ads to those people you suspect make up your target audience. But as you receive more visitors and likes on your page, you'll be growing your own data set, and from that you can better determine what kinds of people you actually attract and better refine the parameters when creating subsequent ads.

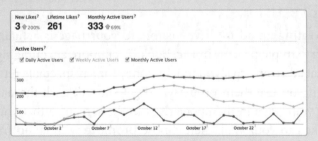

Cross referencing active users with your status updates can help you determine what your customers are most attracted to.

To start, open up your page **insights** through the link found either on your edit page (see p.100) or within the shortcuts displayed on your page's wall (see p.106). You'll first see an overview of **user activity** – a tally of how many people visit your page over time – along with a graph of **interactions** – a calculation of how often individual posts are viewed and commented on. These broad numbers give you a general sense of traffic for your page, but the more interesting data lies behind the **see details** links.

The details inside insights are certainly useful, providing a list of your most popular posts within a defined time range, but it's user activity details that will give you the best overview of your fan base. Not only can you measure activity against insights (e.g., likes per visit), you're also given a breakdown of your fans' **demographics**: gender, age, the countries and cities where they live, the languages they speak and what particular tab (see p.109) they explore the most. You're also given stats on how often fans watch your movies, look at your photos or listen to any music you suggest. The next time you're looking to buy an ad, be sure to dip into these numbers to get a sense of where your money will best be spent!

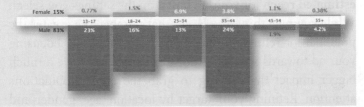

	0.77%	1.5%	6.9%	3.8%	1.1%	0.30%
Female 15%						
	13–17	18–24	25–34	35–44	45–54	55+
Male 83%	23%	16%	13%	24%	1.9%	4.2%

method in place to charge for their service, see p.97 for more on payments), before being presented with a page full of options that will help you define your ad.

First you'll need to determine where people interested in your ad will be taken if they click it. If you have an outside website (see p.144), you can choose **external url** and enter your web address as the destination, otherwise select your page from the drop-down list. Next, select the **type** of ad you want to run. You can create a traditional

The list of shortcuts on your page's wall provides quick access to your advertisements and insights (see p.104).

ad that includes a short message alongside your page's profile pic, or you can choose the **sponsored story** model, which uses your fans' support as an advertisement in and of itself.

> **TIP:** Return to your active (or inactive) ads at any time by following this link: www.facebook.com/ads/manage

Now you've got to decide who are your target audience. You'll notice a box along the side of the page that suggests the **estimated reach** for your ad based on the settings you select. While you may think the larger that number, the greater the potential for return, in fact it's quite the opposite. Focusing your ad towards specific groups of people can have a much bigger impact than trying to grab the entire population's attention. Refining your target by location, age, gender and interests not only allows you to create ads that will resonate with specific groups, but will **cost less**, too. See the box on p.104–5 for ways to determine exactly which targets are currently worth your effort.

> **TIP:** When determining which **interests** to include as part of your ad's target demographics, avoid top-level subjects in favour of smaller, related terms. For example, the interest "football" will yield a very large pool of fans, though they're more likely to skip over yet another football ad. While "goalie" reduces the overall number of football enthusiasts, it lets you focus your advert towards that specific, probabilistically more interested group.

Once you're focused on whom you want to reach, it's time to set how long your ad will run and how much you're willing to spend. Begin by **naming** your campaign something that will remind you of the particular demographics you chose – this way you can more easily check back on what worked best when designing future campaigns. Next set an upper limit for the amount you're willing to pay over the life of your ad, set a schedule for how long it will run and choose whether you'd like to **pay by impression** or **pay by click** – the difference is subtle, yet important. Buying

CultFootball

Footy news unfit for print. Come share your thoughts about the beautiful game!

👍 Like · Sean Mahoney likes this.

Ads are limited to 25 characters for the title and 135 characters for the body text, though you can upload any size image you'd like (otherwise it will default to your page's profile pic).

ads by impression means you will pay just for the placement of your ad on a page, while paying by click means you'll get similar exposure but only pay when someone actually clicks on your ad.

Paying by click is generally recommended, unless you're looking for wide-ranging brand exposure and don't care about click-through (a model very much like traditional print and television advertising, where you attempt to create a **subconscious association** in the consumer's mind by bombarding them with your brand). You should be aware that if you receive a lot of hits using the pay-by-click option, you will run through your budget more quickly. This, though, is a happy problem, since it means your campaign has generated a great response.

> **TIP:** Check on impressions and click numbers by visiting your ad account page at www.facebook.com/ads/manage and selecting **reports** from the menu on the left.

Social plug-ins

Maintaining a website for your business is pretty much a necessity in this day and age (if you don't have one yet, see our picks on p.144). Just as you're bound to suggest friends from your Facebook page visit your website from time to time, you can also nudge your website visitors back towards your Facebook account using ready-made **plug-ins**.

Page tabs

Though the majority of interaction with your fans will take place on your wall, you may want to set aside space for things like contests or **coupons**. This is best accomplished by creating new **tabs** within your page, then filling those tabs with the content you want to share.

Take a look on the left of your window and you'll see a sidebar similar to the one on your personal home page (see p.52). The icons already here, like photos and info, correspond with subpages – or tabs – within your main page. You can create as many tabs as you'd like, though it isn't exactly a straightforward affair. If you have some experience working with HTML, do a search for **static html** in Facebook's search bar, and use Mensing and Padvorac's app to get started (theirs is the one with 57 million fans). If you have no experience working with HTML or web design, use one of the following services to help create your new tabs. These will also lend support for creating contests, importing blog posts, designing a mini website right in Facebook and enabling a **fan gate**, where new visitors to your site will have to "like" you in order to get past the welcome screen:

▶ **Wildfire:** http://iframes.wildfireapp.com

▶ **Involver Static HTML:** www.involver.com/applications

▶ **Iwipa:** www.facebook.com/iwipa

▶ **FaceItPages:** www.faceitpages.com

You're sure to have seen Facebook "like" buttons on sites around the web, and we've already explored how **Facebook Connect** lets people sign in to third-party sites using their Facebook credentials (see p.81). You can accomplish all of this yourself by pasting a little bit of HTML code into just the right place inside your website. And though this may tip over into the "advanced" category, Facebook and the

Facebook Marketplace, powered by Oodle, lets you list your wares for sale, and posts automatic alerts to your page's wall.

website creators we suggested on the previous page provide good support, and the initial struggle will be well worth the effort when you see your page's likes on the rise.

Find your way to http://developers.facebook.com/docs/plugins and you'll be presented with a plethora of plug-in options. For each, you'll need to fill in a few fields to let Facebook know how you'd like the plug-in to look on your website. Once you've got it configured, click **get code**, then copy and paste it into the appropriate place in your website (check your website service's FAQs to determine best placement).

29,734 people like this. Be the first of your friends.

Plug-ins let you add a like button to your website, so people can instantly join your following without having to search for you in Facebook. They make sending a comment from website to timeline a snap, and let you include a recent activity box, encourage visitors to recommend your website to friends and enable log in using Facebook usernames and passwords.

Twitter

Twitter
Shorter, faster, stronger

Once upon a time there was the telegram, in its day considered the very height of communications technology. Messages could be transmitted with electric speed from station to station, where operators sat patiently transcribing dots and dashes into common language. But the medium demanded a new way of writing, focused on specifics conveyed in as few words as possible. Two hundred years later we find ourselves presented with very similar conditions (though without all those messy wires).

Taking its cue from the speed of mobile text messaging, while adhering to the same 140 character count limit, **Twitter** has built a social network based around short, timely bursts of information. Better known as **tweets**, these communications are amazingly useful for sharing alerts and warnings, quickly directing people to a website or physical location and staying in touch with unfolding events as they happen throughout the world. You can follow whomever you want, and anyone can follow you, making it less about who you are and more about what you have to say.

Getting started

As far as social media services go, Twitter is one of the easiest to set up. Direct your web browser to www.twitter. com and fill in your name, email address and a password (if you'd like to establish separate email accounts for personal and professional use, see p.22 for a list of our top providers). Then it's on to choosing a username, verifying your account, finding people to follow… but let's not get ahead of ourselves.

What's in a name?

As soon as you're past the first screen you'll be asked to choose a **username**. While you're limited to upper and lowercase letters, numbers and the underscore symbol, you do not have to use a real word or even come close to your actual name. Your username, or **Twitter handle**, can be clever, punchy, suggest a dominant personality trait, allude to a much loved hobby, match up with a product or business – whatever you'd like. And if you can't find just the right expression of your inner self at the moment, don't stress too much – you have the option of changing it at any time (see p.116).

Twitter encourages you to start following people right away and will ask you to choose from a list of some of the most followed people and organizations on the site. Subscribing to any of these **Twitterati** will include their tweets in your

Twitter feed, or you can **skip this step** by clicking the tiny text prompt at the bottom of the list. As an alternative to the ready-made list, use the **search bar** across the top of the Twitter window to directly identify people more of your ilk.

With so few checks in place, minor identity fraud can plague celebrities and corporations on Twitter. To determine if you're following the actual person or institution as intended, look for the blue verified logo next to their name. Contact Twitter directly if you find yourself being misrepresented.

Following this first round of encouragement, there is another push from Twitter to start following, with **interests** rather than individuals being offered up to draw your attention, before you're taken to the familiar process of adding users found within your email address book (see p.29). Twitter won't save your email password or share your contacts with outside businesses, and this routine does make finding people a whole lot quicker. You're also able to grant Twitter permission to pick through your instant message friends and LinkedIn connections (see p.177). If you're not feeling up to sharing now, you can always return to the option later (see p.133).

The last step is to **verify** your account, which you'll do by replying to an email sent to the address you provided at the start. You don't need to do this instantly, but you will be restricted from some features before you convince Twitter that you're no fake.

Adjust your settings

Twitter's minimalist messaging backbone makes it well suited for mobile phones (see p.138), but it's on your desktop that you'll control your personal information, choose a profile picture and revise the design of your home page. You'll also be given some options to make Twitter a little more private (see p.118) and to manage which outside applications can access your data (see p.146).

Practicalities

Along the top of your Twitter page you'll see a control strip, with a head and shoulders icon sat to the right. Click the icon to reveal a drop-down menu, then select **settings** to open a new screen displaying your **account settings**.

If you ever become dissatisfied with your original handle, here's where you can change the **username** you selected during setup. Twitter will continue collecting tweets from the people you followed under your old name, and your handle will be automatically updated in the feeds of your own followers – though it's a good idea to send out a message (see p.123) letting everyone know about the change,

The option to log out of your account is found under the head and shoulders icon.

otherwise you'll appear to be some random person showing up in their feed.

Within account settings, you'll also find the option of adding an alternate email address where you'll receive your Twitter **notifications** (see p.120). If you'd like to make that address invisible to Twitter searches, untick the button below it. Any changes to your time zone and preferred tweeting **language** – especially handy when you'd like to send the same message to different sets of readers – are also made here.

Twitter also lets you tag your tweets with a location, useful to certain location-based apps (see p.248) though otherwise just some extra information you may want to share with your followers. You'll have the option of adding your location on a tweet-by-tweet basis, but if the idea of having

@QueenRania
Rania Al Abdullah ✓

يوم مشرق في عمان، جلست مع مجموعة من معلمينا.. رغم قلة الموارد في مدارسهم إلا أن #ReformJo حبهم لمهنتهم عطاء لا ينضب

2 Nov via web
☆ Favorite ⇄ Retweet ↩ Reply

Tweets can be written in most major languages, though Twitter handles and hashtags (see p.126) remain exclusively in English.

your movements potentially tracked upsets you, change the **location** option here in your account settings.

Before moving on, take a minute to consider what manner of content you want filling your feed. Twitter will not censor language, nor any attached images or video (see p.130), so you may find yourself looking at some rather interesting selections from time to time. If you don't mind

Privacy

Twitter encourages sharing your thoughts with anyone willing to listen, so discovering that your tweets can be read by everyone – followers or not – shouldn't come as much of a surprise. But if you maintain an account specifically for communicating with a closed group, you'll probably want to lock out potential eavesdroppers.

Head to your **account settings** and make your way to the bottom of the page, where you'll find the option to **protect my tweets**. With this feature enabled, your tweets will only be visible to your followers, and anyone trying to follow you will need to ask your permission first. You'll 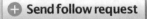 have the chance to approve or disapprove of any new follower requests each time you return to Twitter, and you'll also be sent an email just in case you miss the prompt. As one additional layer of protection, followers will not be able to retweet any of your messages (see p.137).

Account	>
Password	>
Mobile	>
Notifications	>
Profile	>
Design	>
Apps	>

Twitter's settings page is navigable by way of a column of choices along its left side. Clicking a selection will reveal a new page with even more options for controlling how your Twitter account looks and behaves.

the occasional dirty joke or graphic image, select the option to **display media that may contain sensitive content**, and if you're the one who'll be sending out the raunchy tweets, be sure to mark your own media as containing sensitive content. Failing to properly warn people can get you **flagged** and may result in Twitter imposing a permanent R-rating on your account – if that's the case, followers will have to bypass a warning page anytime they want to see one of your tweets.

Give a little more

Twitter isn't intended to be a repository of your life's accomplishments (for that, see Facebook's timeline on p.60), it just allows you to let people know what's happening this very instant. But part of the meaning in your messages comes from context, so providing some short description of who you are can lend a touch of depth to your tweets.

Again within your account settings, choose the profile tab and you'll see fields to fill with your proper name, current location and space for a 160-character bio. If you maintain a website or blog (see p.149), you can enter that info here, too. You'll have also noticed an egg set against a sky blue field accompanying your handle around the page. This profile picture is called an **avatar**, and is the visual representation of your persona on Twitter. Everything on Twitter being compact, your photo will be automatically sheared off at the edges to fit a small square, making it a good idea to choose a horizontal photo with its focus smack in the centre. And because it will become so small (especially on mobile phones, see p.138), you should consider selecting a photo that isn't overly complicated,

Keeping with its avian theme, Twitter starts you out with an egg avatar, presumably to encourage you to break out of your shell.

with simple shapes, vibrant colours and a stark contrast between foreground and background objects. A **headshot**, for instance, will stand out better against a light-coloured background than cropped from a group shot taken in a dimly lit pub. For some tips about getting the best out of your photographs, including referrals to online image-editing programs, see p.68.

> **TIP:** Change how frequently you receive emails from Twitter within the **notifications** tab on the **account settings** page. Here you'll be able to adjust alerts for when you're sent a message (see p.125), when someone new starts following you or when one of your tweets is marked as a favourite (see p.137). You'll also have the option of unsubscribing from Twitter's corporate alerts.

Add some design

Continuing the bird motif, your default Twitter background will appear to be layers of puffy clouds over clear sky. This is just one of a number of **themes** Twitter makes available, along with some easy-to-use colour adjustment tools and the option of uploading your own image as a background. Within your account settings choose **design**, and pick the new theme you'd like to employ. Themes use a combination of a single image, which always originates at the upper left-hand corner of your browser window, and a complementary background colour to create a smooth overall appearance.

You're certainly not limited to using Twitter's available themes. You can **upload** your own 1500 × 1300 pixel background image, and adjust the colours for text, links and the sidebar (see p.134) to create your own unique look. Or, keeping in mind that background images always start

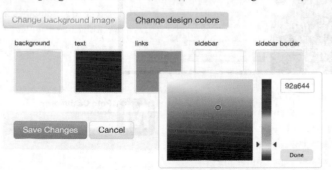

The colour control panel appears after selecting **change design colours**, allowing for greater precision when adjusting the look of your page.

in the same place, you might try your hand at creating a narrow, vertical image that sits on the left, then selecting a Twitter background colour to make it look like your image extends across the entire page. If editing your own images and matching background colours is outside your comfort zone, there are some free online services that can help give your page some pizzazz with much less effort:

▸ **Themeleon:** www.colourlovers.com/themeleon

▸ **Free Twitter Designer:** www.freetwitterdesigner.com

▸ **Tweety Got Back:** www.tweetygotback.com

▸ **TwitBacks:** www.twitbacks.com

Hicks Design, based in Oxfordshire, uses a small vertical image of their logo combined with a black Twitter background to create a seamless effect.

Hugely popular social media news site mashable.com has included their Facebook and YouTube addresses as part of their background.

Tweeting

Tweets are short messages limited to 140 characters each. Just as the sharp chirps of a bird convey a variety of meaning with the slightest change in intonation, so too can tweets paint powerful pictures while adhering to a strict economy of language (see overleaf) – though it does help to use shorthand (see p.140) and the occasional symbol (see p.126) from time to time.

Make yourself heard

Tweeting is just about the easiest form of communication on the Internet. Tweets can't be very long, so it's OK for you to fire off fractions of thoughts the instant they strike. You can tweet from just about anywhere if you have a mobile phone (see p.138), where the character limit actually plays in your favour. And while you may send the occasional **direct message** to specific people (see p.125), your public tweets would have to number in the dozens-per-day range to even begin to irk your followers. This, of course, doesn't mean you should tweet absolute nonsense, just that you needn't limit your enthusiasm too much when the mood strikes.

Click the new tweet icon found along the top of your Twitter page to send out a tweet while viewing just about any part of Twitter.

Respect your limits

When you send your first tweet, it's likely to be along the lines of, "Hello world, I'm finally on Twitter!" And with that brief entrée you'll have used up 25 percent of your character limit. Twitter was conceived as a social **text messaging** network, and as such needed to work on mobile phones, where providers will cut off any text longer than 160 characters. After reserving twenty spaces for a user's handle, we're left with 140 – Twitter's upper limit.

Sceptics suggest that this trend toward brevity is the result of generations of increasingly waning attention spans, but tweets may be best appreciated as part collective thought, part jumping-off point. Noticing that a term is **trending** (see p.134) or seeing a mention of a news event can prompt you to learn more. And as you start composing more messages to your followers, you'll discover that there's actually an art to it. The limited space means you have to make your message concise while still hitting all the right notes, and that requires a specialized sense of rhythm and timing.

If you really must use more than 140 characters (perhaps you're replying to a customer's query, see p.143), there are some services that will take your tweet, cut it off at the limit, then post the rest on an outside website:

▶ **LongReply:** www.longrep.ly

▶ **Jumbo Tweet:** www.jumbotweet.com

▶ **XLTweet:** www.xltweet.com

What's happening?

Who says the Queen has no power? They're rearranging Rio+20 global super-event to avoid clash with her tea party!

⊕ London, England   26 Tweet

A counter keeps track of how many characters you have remaining as you type, though clicking the crosshairs and adjusting your location won't be calculated as part of the final tally.

Click either the new tweet icon or head to your **home** page using the navigation bar at the top of the Twitter window, and start typing in the box with the "Compose new Tweet…" prompt. Choose your location if you've enabled that feature (see p.117), and when you're done, hit **tweet**. As simple as that, you've joined the hundreds of millions of people spreading messages, crucial and mundane, across the globe.

DMs and @mentions

Tweets you send to the public may be intended for your followers, but by default they can be seen by anyone, even people without a Twitter account. But you can also send direct messages (abbreviated in the twitterverse as DMs) to people in private. Click the head and shoulders icon, select **Direct messages**, then tap the **New message** button to open a regular-looking tweet window – only this time you can select to send a secure note to any of your followers. As one

added layer of privacy, you can't send
a DM to someone who doesn't follow
you, and in order for them to write back,
they'll have to follow you in return. All of
your DMs will be saved in your message page,
and you can return and pick up the thread at any time.

> **TIP:** Twitter supports many symbols that you won't find on any keyboard. Web services like www.twsym.com and http://thenextweb/twitterkeys provide long lists of symbols you can use in your tweets with a simple cut and paste.

Working in similar fashion to DMs, but including absolutely no privacy checks, are **@mentions**. These are effectively shout-outs to anyone on Twitter with whom you'd like to engage in conversation (not that they have to reciprocate). You don't need to follow a person to @mention them in a tweet, and they won't need to follow you either. If you're ever mentioned in another person's tweet you'll receive a notice under the **@Connect** tab on your home page.

Searches and #hashtags

You're able to search for people by name, Twitter handle or email using the search field at the top of your Twitter page, though once you've identified and started **following** them (see p.132) you won't have any need to search for them again. But you need not restrict yourself to collecting Tweeters with your searches – you can ask

Twitter to comb through its entire archive of tweets to locate mentions of any subject, fact or person, fictional or historical. And if you find yourself looking up the same terms over and over, save yourself some time by having Twitter remember them. Simply click the gear icon that appears on the search results page and choose to **save your search**. Now, whenever you click inside the search field on your home page, you'll see a list of all your saved terms.

While there are no limits on the terms or phrases you can use when tweeting (save for character count), there's a convention unique to Twitter that encourages tagging important terms with a hashmark. Starting with the # symbol, these **hashtags** are used by Tweeters to add their tweets to the same subject thread. Hashtags can provide added context or be used as a point of emphasis, and are separated from common usage of the same words within search results. And clicking on any hashtag term will take you to a list of every public tweet using that same tag.

By default, your home page displays tweets from everyone you follow, but you can change the view using the icons found in the control strip at the top of the page. @**Connect** displays all your messages and @mentions; #**Discover** reveals popular stories, highlights recent activity among the Tweeters you follow and suggests new people you may want to add (see p.132); and **Home** brings you back to where it all started.

Hashtags, by design, are comprised of only one word – but clever tweeters have taken to combining terms to create **super words**. Using a mixture of lower and uppercase letters, you can merge phrases into words while keeping a reasonable level of readability. Sometimes these mashed together creations become so well known that acronyms emerge, maintaining meaning while saving precious space (as it was in the case of #OccupyWallStreet becoming the more common #OWS).

> **TIP:** Though TYPING IN ALL CAPS is generally read as shouting, Twitter categorizes entirely capitalized phrases in much the same way as it does hashtags – the advantage being that you can use spaces in between words.

Shortening URLs

More than anything else, social media is about sharing. While some of us may lead such exciting lives that we can just relay our daily activities, most of us will want to share our thoughts about the things we've seen and read. That, though, requires context, more often than not provided by way of a **web link**.

By now you more than understand how little room you have when constructing a tweet, so the last thing you need is a sprawling web address taking up precious character space. Not to fear, Twitter will automatically shorten your link to twenty characters, and subtract that amount from

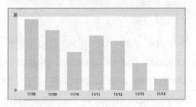

Click analytics, like the offerings from Fur.ly and Su.pr, often take the form of infographics. In this example, a simple bar graph tracks the number of clicks over time.

the live character tally as you type. There are also a number of online **URL shortening** services that will do the same thing, but offer additional features like click analytics (which reveal how many people followed your link to its source) and the ability to combine multiple links into one shortened address. It's as simple as copying the address of the webpage you're viewing, navigating to one of the services listed below and pasting it into their shortening engine. Then copy and paste the result into your tweet, and when someone clicks on it, they'll be taken to the original page as you'd intended:

▶ **bit.ly:** http://bitly.com

▶ **fur.ly:** http://fur.ly

▶ **Google URL shortener:** http://goo.gl

▶ **Su.pr (by StumbleUpon):** http://su.pr

Google's shortening service will record who clicked your link by date, location, device and operating system. They also create a **QR code** for your long link. Useful for business promotions (see p.143), copying your QR code into an email newsletter or print advertising will allow smartphone owners to scan it and be sent directly to your link.

Photos

Beyond your insights and web links, you're bound to want to share the occasional photo with your followers. Because Twitter is a text-only system, you won't be able to display them right in your message (though some smartphone Twitter apps have found a workaround, see p.141). Instead, they'll appear as a web link so that anyone reading your tweet can click the link and be to sent to a separate webpage where Twitter keeps a copy of the image.

Start by typing a new tweet as you normally would – it's always a good idea to include some sort of context for any images or links – then click the camera icon along the bottom of your tweet's window and search your computer for an image. When you've found the one you want, choose select or open, and Twitter will do the rest. You're only allowed one photo per tweet, so if you

Tweets with pictures are indicated by a tiny photo icon in the Twitter timeline; clicking the icon displays the full-sized image. Making a tweet a favourite (see p.137) lights up its corner with a golden star.

don't like what you've chosen simply click the tiny "×" in its upper right-hand corner to delete the image and begin anew.

Videos

Twitter may support photo uploads in your tweets, but they don't currently provide the same sort of easy solution for videos. That's not to say they discourage you from sharing videos – on the contrary, videos attached to tweets appear in the sidebar just as photos do, and even receive their own icon. You'll just have to use an outside service to make it all work.

Twitter has preferred video partners (listed below) that make the whole operation run quite smoothly. If you want to share your own homemade video, you'll need to sign up for one of these services separately, but if you just want to pass along something you've seen while browsing, find the **share** button near the video you're watching and click the icon for Twitter. You'll either be prompted to sign into your Twitter account, or if you're already logged in, you'll immediately see a tweet window very much like the one you're used to, only this time with a link to the video taking up part of your message. And don't worry about the link's length: all these video services automatically shorten links to twenty characters.

▶ **YouTube:** www.youtube.com (see p.262)

▶ **Vimeo:** www.vimeo.com

▶ **Twitvid:** www.twitvid.com

▶ **Justin.tv:** www.justin.tv

▶ **Ustream:** www.ustream.tv

Following

With your account humming along and the whole tweeting thing well within your control, you'll want to start finding more people to fill your feed with updates. Twitter helpfully provides some ways for you to find new additions, taking into account the people you already follow and anyone whose Twitter page you've recently viewed. They'll also suggest people followed by the people you follow, and toss the occasional promoted account in the mix. Head to your Twitter **home** page and we'll take a look at the method behind this madness.

Who to follow

One of the easiest ways of finding new Tweeters is through Twitter's **who to follow** tool. You'll see a mini representation of the tool's results in the sidebar of your home page (see p.134), but to use its full functionality you'll need to click the **#Discover** icon found in the navigation bar at the top of your Twitter page.

You're presented with a list of possibles who are currently followed by people you follow, the assumption being if you like someone, you're sure to like the people

Twitter isn't above selling ad space, though what free-to-use service is? Whenever you see an arrow icon like the one to the right, it means some one or some thing has paid to promote that tweet.

they like too. The list is peppered with promoted Tweeters and Twitterati, though for the most part the suggestions will have a connection to at least two people you've previously chosen

to follow. Give it a scan, and if you find someone interesting click the **follow** button next to her handle. From now on, that author's tweets will appear in your feed.

A slightly more hands-on method of finding new people is to search for them by subject. Click **Browse categories** at the bottom of the list, and you'll have the choice of exploring Tweeters within the arts, business, entertainment, fashion, government… the list goes on. You'll only see top Tweeters, ranked according to how engaged they are with their followers (rather than by their number of followers), and from there you can add them in the same way as before.

> **TIP:** To **unfollow** someone, navigate to your following page using the link at the top of your sidebar (see overleaf), and hover your mouse over the green following button until it turns red and says unfollow. Click once, and they're gone.

The final option for identifying new Tweeters is one you first saw when signing up for your account – granting Twitter access to your email address books (see p.115). Select **find friends** next to the browse interests tab, and give Twitter permission to locate people you know who already use the service. Following friends is also bound to secure some new followers for yourself (see p.143).

The sidebar

Once you're following a few dozen people, Twitter's website can start to feel like a scroll of endless tweets coming in faster than you can keep track. It's easy to get lost in the feed, so to help provide some perspective, Twitter reminds us of some of its other features inside a **sidebar** off to the left. Beyond condensing the activity in your tiny corner of the twitterverse, the sidebar displays **trending topics**, suggests Tweeters for you to follow and provides links to lists of people with whom you're currently connected.

As useful as it is in its original form, the sidebar isn't a static element bound to its home page duties. Clicking through to your personal profile page transforms the sidebar into a navigation tool, letting you easily switch between your tweets, followers, favourites (see p.137) and lists (see p.136). It also collects a sampling of recent photos and videos you've shared. When you find yourself on someone else's profile page, the sidebar provides the same information for that person and also includes a handy **direct message** feature (see p.125).

Trending topics get special treatment too – selecting any link in the **trends** list fills your timeline with recent tweets that include the trending tag or phrase, while the sidebar displays the most popular Tweeters involved with the trend alongside related photos and videos. The full list of trending topics remains available, so you can switch between them without having to click back to your home page.

Clicking **tweets** takes you to your profile page, where your full list of tweets is displayed.

See everyone you're following or all of your followers on one page, or **compose** a new tweet without opening another window (see p.123).

Click the "×" to remove unwanted suggestions from the **Who to follow** tool's mini feed, and you'll be helping Twitter better determine the people you see in the future.

Trending topics can be adjusted to focus on specific countries and cities across the globe, though promoted hashtags (see p.132) remain consistent.

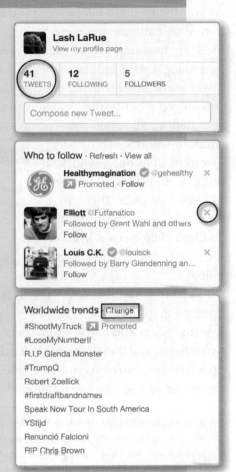

Lash LaRue
View my profile page

41
TWEETS

12
FOLLOWING

5
FOLLOWERS

Compose new Tweet...

Who to follow · Refresh · View all

Healthymagination ✓ @gehealthy ×
↗ Promoted · Follow

Elliott @Futfanatico ×
Followed by Grant Wahl and others
Follow

Louis C.K. ✓ @louisck ×
Followed by Barry Glendenning an...
Follow

Worldwide trends Change

#ShootMyTruck ↗ Promoted
#LoseMyNumberIf
R.I.P Glenda Monster
#TrumpQ
Robert Zoellick
#firstdraftbandnames
Speak Now Tour In South America
YStijd
Renunció Falcioni
RIP Chris Brown

Creating lists

As you follow more people on Twitter, your feed can start to resemble an unmanageable sprawl. Rather than unfollow Tweeters hovering just at your interest threshold (they do pass along a good link every once in a while, after all), you might consider organizing your favourites by list. **Lists** let you curate selections of people under headings that you define, allowing you to check in with (or avoid) select Tweeters all at once. And you don't have to follow someone in order to place them in a list, helping you get around Twitter's **2000-person limit** on the number of people you can follow.

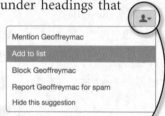

Block Tweeters using the same drop-down panel you use when adding new people to your lists.

To create a new list, select the person's handle so you're taken to their page, then click the tiny head and shoulders icon and select **add to list**. From there you can either **create a new list** or add the person to an existing one. When setting up a new list, you're given the option of leaving it open to the public or keeping it private. Public lists can be seen by

TIP: If you want to stop receiving the retweets passed along by someone you follow, first navigate to their profile page, then click the head and shoulders icon next to the following button and select **Turn off Retweets** from the drop-down menu that appears.

anyone visiting your profile, and if they like what they see, they can also follow the list you created. You'll see a tally of how many Tweeters you've placed in your list, along with the number of people following your list at the top of each one. And following lists works both ways – you're able to follow any **public list** you find on any person's profile page.

➕ **Follow this list**

Checking activity

Rather than focus on what the people you're following have to say, Twitter's activity tracker shows what they've been doing on the site. Click the **#Discover** link at the top of your page, then choose **Activity** in your sidebar and you'll be shown all the latest action in the worlds of the people you follow – from the newest people they've started to follow, to the tweets they've **favourited** or **retweeted**. The activity page is one of the more useful ways of finding new people to follow, as you can see exactly who the people you like find engaging.

SteveMartinToGo Steve Martin
The conquistadors are back, and this time they set up an lemonade stand on my front lawn. Do I call police or simply attack?
1 Nov ☆ Favorite ⇄ Retweet ↰ Reply · Open

Hovering your mouse over any tweet brings up some hidden options. Clicking **Favorite** sends the tweet to a list of your favourites accessed through the **Profile** button at the top of your Twitter window, while clicking **Retweet** will forward it to all your followers alongside a mention of the original author.

Going mobile

Twitter was originally designed to work on mobile phones (see p.124), and while the website provides a robust interface with plenty of customizable functions, the heart of Twitter remains on the go. Twitter's most unique aspect is its immediacy – you're tweeting what's happening in your world as it occurs, and reading about what's happening in the world around you in near-real time. Twitter has scooped news services and provoked social movements, and none of it was restricted to a desktop. Let's explore some of the ways you can take Twitter with you.

Twitter for everyone

Phones weren't quite as smart when Twitter first came online as they are now, and Twitter hasn't forgotten its roots. Anyone that can receive text messages on their mobile can send and receive tweets, though smartphone apps do deliver quite a few more features (see p.141). To begin, head to your **account settings** (see p.116) and click the **mobile** tab. From there, select your country and enter your mobile number. You'll be sent a verification code which you'll have to text back to Twitter. Then, whenever you want to tweet, simply reply to the same number that sent your verification code.

Click the head and shoulders icon on the page of anyone you follow for the option of receiving mobile notifications about their activity.

You're always limited to 140 characters, so using shorthand is often very useful (see overleaf). There's also a specific set of abbreviated commands that will control how Twitter handles your texted tweets, retrieves user information and operates overall (standard text message rates apply):

▶ **@[username] + message:** creates a **public message** to anyone on Twitter (see p.123)

▶ **d [username] + message:** sends a private, **direct message** to anyone you follow (see p.125)

▶ **rt [username]: retweets** that user's most recent tweet

▶ **set location [place]:** updates your **location** to that place

▶ **whois [username]:** sends a user's **profile info** to your mobile

▶ **fav [username]:** marks that user's last tweet as a **favorite**

▶ **on/off:** turns **all** your authorized Twitter **notifications** either on or off

▶ **on/off [username]:** turns on or off notifications from a **single person** that you follow

▶ **follow/unfollow [username]: follows** or **unfollows** a person

▶ **leave [username]: stop** receiving **notifications** from a person without unfollowing them

▶ **help:** asks Twitter to send a list of shorthand commands

TIP: In the US, one number handles everyone's Twitter texts (40404), but in other parts of the world it varies by carrier. Find the appropriate number for your country by typing "short code" into the help search bar, found in **help** under **account settings.**

Mobile shorthand

Whether we like it or not, SMS shorthand has entered common usage. But that doesn't mean we should completely give ourselves over to it in emails and spoken conversation. Better that we use it where it works best – in messages where there are **strict limits** on character count.

By now most of us know that LOL means laugh out loud, or that you can replace the "eight" sound in words like mate or hate with its numerical equivalent (m8, h8) to save space. Other constructions aren't so obvious, but are still used with enough frequency that they're worth knowing and, on occasion, using yourself.

bion: believe it or not

bol: best of luck

brb: be right back

btw: by the way

cd9: "code nine" means parents are nearby

cmn: come on

4e: forever

foaf: friend of a friend

fwiw: for what it's worth

#ff: "follow friday" – use with a list of handles you suggest others follow (only use on Fridays)

ftw: for the win

gg: good game

idk: I don't know

imho: in my humble opinion

irl: in real life

jk: just kidding

lombard: lots of money but a right dick

mt: modified tweet

mtf: more to follow

nsfw: not safe for work

nts: note to self

oic: oh, I see

pm: private message

pwn: humiliated

sys: see you soon

tmb: tweet me back

tmi: too much information

ttyl: talk to you later

tyt: take your time

woz: slang for "was"

wtv: whatever

ykyat: you know you're addicted to…

ymmv: your mileage may vary

yoyo: you're on your own

ztwitt: tweeting extremely quickly

Smartphones

There's very little difference in functionality between Twitter's website and their official **smartphone app**; the only thing they don't share is the same interface. But that's easy to overlook when you can just as easily read your feeds, message friends, find new people to follow, adjust your profile, even upload photos all from your phone. Plus, the action icons used are consistent from website to app, so if you know it on the web, you'll know it on your phone.

To start, make sure you've enabled the mobile feature in the same way you would for plain SMS twittering (see p.138) – if you don't, you'll receive a prompt from your app to change those settings. Then download the Twitter app from the store that supports your phone (there are versions for iPhone, Android, Blackberry and Windows phones), enter your Twitter login information, and watch as your Twitter feed fills with the latest updates from the people you follow.

Twitter's mobile app opens to your entire timeline. Check in on your interactions or direct messages, or search for a username or #hashtag by tapping the icons along the bottom of the screen. The **Me** button contains information about your profile, favourites and lists, as well as your account settings and notification preferences.

The smartphone app market isn't exclusive to Twitter's offering. There are a number of free apps that do what Twitter's does, but include added features and a refined design that can make tweeting from your mobile seem slightly more intuitive. Some even consolidate your Facebook and Twitter accounts into the same app, so you can see what's happening in both worlds and then send updates to each simultaneously. Some of the best include:

▶ **TweetDeck:** www.tweetdeck.com

▶ **TweetCaster:** www.tweetcaster.com

▶ **HootSuite:** www.hootsuite.com

▶ **Echofon:** www.echofon.com

Twitter + Facebook

Twitter has a built-in method for creating Facebook status updates (see p.44) out of your tweets. Head to your **Account Settings** and choose **Profile**. Scroll to the bottom of the page and click the Facebook button to connect your accounts. Now whatever you tweet will become your Facebook status.

There are some disadvantages to sharing accounts in this direction: 1. you shouldn't update your Facebook status as frequently as you tweet, because 2. brevity and spontaneity are encouraged in tweets, but Facebook updates should offer more insight and at least consider grammar. If you tweet more than three times a day, you might try reversing the direction, and send shortened Facebook updates to Twitter using one of the services listed above.

Twitter for business

Finding people to follow is no problem on Twitter (see p.132), but how do you let people know you're out there when you have a product to sell or an organization to promote? Like most things worth the effort, there are no shortcuts to success. And though the process isn't terribly taxing, it will take **time** and **genuine involvement** on your part to build an engaged following.

Encouraging new followers

Following someone on Twitter doesn't demand the sort of mutual acknowledgement that Facebook's friendships do (see p.40), meaning you can follow people without them having to follow you. Yet **reaching out** and following people is still the first, and possibly best, way to encourage people to follow you back. Start by identifying people who work in your field, create similar products or share your tastes, and follow them while simultaneously engaging them using @ mentions (see p.125). Use your @mentions to pose questions,

add comments and suggest real advice to people – the key word being **real**. No one wants to be spammed with web links; they want a real person and real conversations.

London-based web design company Moonfruit famously used a **Twitter contest** to promote their brand and gain more followers. The contest was simple, only requiring people to tweet them @moonfruit while using the #moonfruit hashtag (see p.126) for the chance of winning a Macbook computer.

As more people follow you, their followers will begin to take notice. It's key that you continue the conversation with the people you've already attracted as you reach out in new directions, and that your general tweets are **interesting** and **relevant** – don't just tweet to hear yourself chirp. The goal is to become an authority in your specific area, to be the person that people trust to provide worthwhile insight on a regular basis, all while maintaining that human touch.

> **TIP:** The **Who to follow** tool (see p.132) can help you find people who share your interests. You might also try www.justtweetit.com or www.wefollow.com to search by interest, and www.nearbytweets .com or www.twellow.com to identify people close by.

Twitter resources

If you have a business of any size, chances are you have a **website**. Just as you're sure to tweet your followers about new products or additions to your website from time to time, you'll also want to encourage your website visitors to follow you on Twitter. Happily, Twitter provides some ready-made tools to help create a seamless connection between the two.

Head to www.twitter.com/about/resources or click **Resources** in the fine print at the bottom of your sidebar, and you'll be taken

Though stand-alone websites are just outside the scope of this book, if you don't have one yet we suggest you start with www.wordpress.org or http://sites.google.com.

to a screen with options for downloading a **follow button**, a **tweet button** and some clever little modules called **widgets**. For each, you'll fill in some information about how you want the button or widget to appear, then copy and paste the HTML code into your site (see the help section of your particular website publisher to find out where to paste this code). Though this process does border on "advanced", having a button on your website that lets people immediately follow you on Twitter or tweet what they're seeing with a reference to your website is well worth the time it takes to sort it out.

Analytics

You can spend all day sharing your tweets and encouraging new people to follow you, but unless you take a look at the numbers you'll never fully understand what works and what doesn't (and even then there's a decent amount of interpretation involved). There are more than a few tools to help you track your influence across the

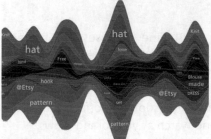

Neofromix.com's **Twitter Stream Graphs** show related words for any single search term, displayed over time – useful for focusing your outreach within a broader subject field.

145

twitterverse, often displaying results in cleverly realized **infographics**. Others are more bare bones, but still get the job done (like www.tweeteffect.com, which lists specific tweets that have increased or decreased your **follower count**). Whatever the case, the best thing you can do is explore the options in the sites listed below and attempt to translate the results into better tweeting practices. If you're getting good feedback from a particular subject thread, or have determined that your users are mostly online for certain hours each day – go with it. Identify your base, continually engage with them and expand from there.

▶ **Twitalyzer:** www.twitalyzer.com

▶ **Tweepi:** www.tweepi.com

▶ **Klout:** www.klout.com

▶ **The Archivist:** http://archivist.visitmix.com

▶ **TweetReach:** www.tweetreach.com

▶ **MentionMapp:** www.mentionmapp.com

Twitter parties

Taking their cue from the online Q&A sessions hosted by major websites, Twitter parties bring people together through a shared hashtag to discuss some specific topic. Announce your event on all your social media accounts, bring in an expert to field questions or offer a prize for joining the discussion, and watch as your brand grows.

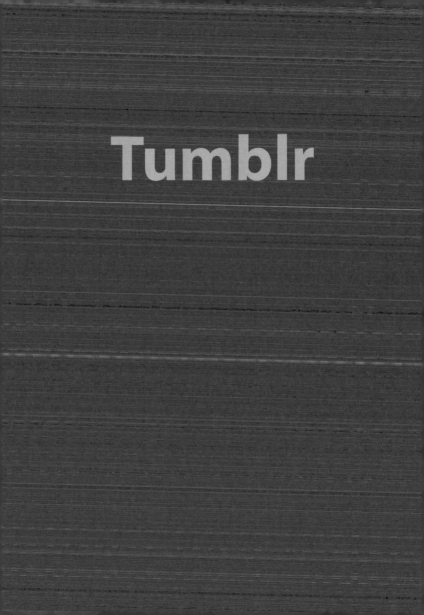

Tumblr

Tumblr
Microblogging for the masses

Web logs, or blogs as they're more commonly known, have been around for over a decade – an eternity in Internet terms. Though blogs encourage long and often elaborate posts, they are in no small part responsible for the birth of services such as Facebook and Twitter, where people share their thoughts and experiences in a much more compact format. In exchange for the easy-to-use features of these big services, we've given up one of the most attractive features of full-fledged blogging – total control over how our page looks on the screen. Tumblr fixes that.

Combining the impetuous brevity of Twitter with the fine visual control offered by blogs, Tumblr has created a highly customizable microblogging platform – so called because the posts are short, not because the service is tiny. It's full of oddities and outside thinkers, though traditional news outlets and conservative pundits number among its members. And because of how easily it accepts photos, video and music, Tumblr has become especially popular with musicians and photographers, while its controls are simple enough for any layman to master.

Take a tumblr

Before you start posting your thoughts and finding other Tumblr bloggers to check in on, you'll have to set up your first tumblr. Head to www.tumblr.com and fill in the boxes with your email address and a password (in the event you'd like to create a new email account just for this purpose, see p.23 for some recommended services). You'll also be asked for a **URL**, which will become your blog's web address. URLs are unique, so chances are your name and other common words will be taken. Anything will do for now – if you're dissatisfied with your first choice, you'll have the chance to change it further down the road (see p.155).

The dashboard

After signing in and completing a CAPTCHA test (see p.29), you'll be taken to your tumblr's **dashboard.** The dashboard is essentially your home page, the place from which you'll originate posts (see p.158) and read all the new content coming in from the people you follow (see box on p.157). Here too is where you'll find your way to all the settings that make Tumblr so adaptable (without being too overwhelming). Though before you start showing yourself off to the community, there's a bit of housekeeping to attend to.

Clicking the Tumblr logo at the top of your page will always return you to your dashboard.

Like all social media services, Tumblr encourages you to choose a single photo as your visual representation around the site. This photo, called an **avatar**, will accompany your likes and questions on other people's tumblrs, and will become the link to your own tumblr for anyone choosing to follow you. Begin by clicking on the default, blank-faced avatar. You'll be taken to a page full of **settings** with the prompt to upload a photo right at the top – any will do, but square jpegs larger than 128 × 128 pixels work best. Select **browse,** choose an image from your computer, then scroll down past the rest

Your tumblr's avatar also becomes your **favicon** – the tiny image to the left of the URL in your web browser's address bar.

of the options on the page (we'll return to those later, see p 155) and click **save preferences**. With that, you've taken the first step towards standing out amongst all the other tumblrs online.

TIP: After your first avatar is uploaded, clicking on it from your dashboard will send you directly to your public tumblr page – as seen by someone visiting your site – rather than the settings page you were taken to when you clicked the default image. From now on you can only change your avatar within your settings (see p.155).

Tumblr won't automatically update the dashboard the same way Facebook does with its news feed (see p.42). Instead, you'll see an alert appear at the top of your page whenever someone you follow posts a new entry.

Customize it

Tumblr has made it amazingly easy to create posts from all sorts of text and media (see p.158), and nearly as easy to redesign your page. From your dashboard, click **Untitled** at the top of the screen and you'll be taken to the control page for your tumblr. It just so happens that "Untitled" is the rather uninspired default name of your new tumblr, but we're about to fix that and show you how to make your blog look much prettier in the process.

Appearances matter

Besides the recent activity displayed in the centre of the page, you'll see very little difference between your dashboard view and what appears on screen after you click "Untitled". The important difference is found on the right, in your **sidebar**. Along with a URL link to the public view of your tumblr, and some buttons to help you manage your posts (see p.160), you'll see an option to **customize appearance**. Behind that is an amazing array of features that will help you make your blog look practically any way you'd like it to.

Your customizing screen is divided into two columns – a narrow left-hand column where you're presented with settings that control the appearance of your blog, and a wider right-hand column that shows a preview of the changes as you make them. You're also given the option of revising the **name** of your tumblr from "Untitled" to anything you'd like (so long as it's less that fifty characters), and adding a description about what you're planning to post.

While adjusting fonts and background colours are pretty simple skills to master, and combined with your **theme** (see overleaf) provide enough customization for most people, uploading your own **header** and **background** isn't quite as straightforward. Each of these should take the form of an image file and be no wider than 875 pixels (see our image editing suggestions on p.68). The background will be fixed behind your posts and spread through the entire page. But because your header is intended to sit only at the top, it should be significantly less

The appearance sidebar provides the option of displaying who you follow on your tumblr page. It also lets you turn on or off the tags associated with your posts (see p.164), include album covers from songs you upload (see p.162) and create a "see more" link for posts that become overly long. You can also add subpages under your main page – useful for when tangents become full-blown themes.

153

tall than it is wide – though there is no formal restriction on its height. And because it will be placed above your tumblr's standard title, you'll want to include some text treatment or **logo** in your image to let people know where they've arrived.

> **TIP:** Header and background images smaller than 875 pixels wide will cause the image to repeat, creating a series of tiles across the page. While this isn't recommended for your header, using a small background image can create a stylish **mosaic** effect.

Themes

Above the settings panel you'll notice what looks like a tiny copy of your current page design. This is a representation of your **theme** (by default, something called "redux"). If simply adjusting colours and fonts isn't enough, click the **themes** button at the very top of the sidebar and pick a new design to change both the colour scheme and layout of your entire page.

There are many free themes to choose from, and some that may have you reaching for your credit card. Before you decide on one, you should consider what sort of content you'll most frequently post. For example, photographers may want to use a theme whose

⬇ Install Theme

Some page designers like to share their work. If you come across a homemade tumblr with a look that you love, click the **install theme** button in the upper right to take its design as your own.

layout allows for multiple images across the page, while writers might go for a more literary style, with columns against a clean background for easy reading. You should also take a look at your **appearance sidebar** after choosing a theme – some themes include features beyond the standard set, like displaying Facebook and Twitter buttons, while others provide multiple colour selectors that allow you to adjust the entire palette of your page.

Settings

Now that your tumblr looks the way you'd like it to, it's time to make sure it behaves itself in a manner befitting its newly polished appearance. From your dashboard, click the name of your tumblr at the top of the page (previously known as "Untitled") and choose **settings** from the sidebar that appears. You'll remember this page from when you changed your **avatar** (see p.151). Now let's address the remaining options.

Though icons usually remain consistent in both look and function throughout a website, there's one exception on Tumblr. The gear icon along the top of your screen will take you to your account **preferences** (see p.171) instead of your tumblr's settings.

If you don't like your original **URL** you can rename it here. You can also arrange to use a custom domain name instead of the default construction offered by Tumblr (click the tiny question mark for detailed instructions). To maintain consistency across sites, you may want to use your Twitter handle (see p.114) or the name in your Facebook page's custom URL to complete your tumblr's URL.

You'll also be given the option of changing your dashboard's language, adjusting your time zone, choosing whether you'd

Sharing comments

Tumblr isn't interested in conventional online conversations. Instead of registering yet another opinion within a long string of comments, they encourage you to **reblog** posts you like (see p.169) and to add your thoughts as part of the reblogging process. This may contribute to the idea of "sharing what you find", but it's not great when people want to engage with you directly. For that, you'll have to enable a few functions within your tumblr's **settings**.

The most traditional option, and the one closest to something like Facebook's comments (see p.46), is **replies**. Enabling replies from people who follow your tumblr, or whose tumblrs you follow, allows them to write no more than 250 characters in response to your posts. You'll see their comments in your dashboard feed, and their words will show up under the post for everyone to see.

Though there's no messaging system in Tumblr, you can turn on **questions**, which creates a link to a new page within your tumblr where anyone can write to you on the side. You'll receive an email alert when you receive a question (which you can turn on or off in your preferences, see p.171), and can like search engines (like Google) to be able to comb through your tumblr, and of automatically sharing your posts to **Twitter** and **Facebook**. With the exception of turning on Facebook and Twitter sharing by providing the relevant login information, it's generally a good idea to leave these settings as they are.

send back an answer in private, or publish your response as a new post. Allowing questions is particularly helpful when using Tumblr for your business, where posting answers to common questions

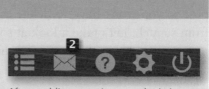

After enabling questions or submissions, you'll see an envelope icon appear along the control strip at the top of your dashboard. New communications result in an alert bubble demanding your response.

might be helpful to all the people that follow you.

You're also able to open your tumblr up to **submissions**. Turn these on, suggest some guidelines to keep people from going too far off track, and they'll be able to send you full posts which you can edit and publish in your own tumblr. By default, opening submissions allows people to post every type of media they could post in their own tumblrs. If you'd like to set some limits, untick the **allowed post types** at the foot of the submissions settings. You can also create submission tags to help return more accurate results for visitors searching your tumblr's history.

Blogging

A pretty design can only get you so far – it's your content that will keep people coming back for more. Tumblr has made it very easy to post all manner of words, images, videos and music to your site. They've also built in systems to manage the timing of your posts, and to allow you to edit an existing post so you won't have to delete the whole thing and start from scratch. Let's take a look at some of the ways you can use your tumblr to share what's going on in your world.

Text posts

Blogging got its start with the written word, and it's words more than anything else that spark controversy and spur conversation. Tumblr lets you write what you want, when you want, and provides a **formatting toolbar** so it will all look the way you want as well. Simply click the text icon on either your dashboard or the control page for your tumblr, and you'll be given a box in which to type. Remember, though there is no official character limit on posts, keeping it short is encouraged. Feel free to upload photos using the link above the box (grabbing a corner of the photo will let

Don't fill your front page with a single, long piece. Click this icon to add a "read more" link in the middle of longer posts. Readers who click the link will be taken to a stand-alone page where your post will be displayed in its entirety.

you **resize** it), and when you're ready, hit **publish** to send your new post to your tumblr. If you want to check your post before making it public, click **preview** and you'll be shown exactly how it will look on your page.

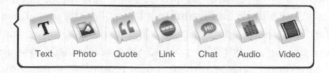

Text   Photo   Quote   Link   Chat   Audio   Video

Tumblr *wants* you to blog. The blogging panel is displayed on your dashboard and on the control page for all your blogs (see p.163 for more on creating multiple blogs), making it easy to post whenever the mood strikes. Clicking any icon will open a new page with unique options for that type of post.

Photo posts

Yes, you can add photos inside text posts, but only the ones currently stored on your computer. Besides, sometimes you just want to share a photo without having to add a description.

Click the photo icon on your blogging panel and you can upload up to ten photos under 10MB each, control their layout, write individual captions and provide a description for the entire set. If you don't have already have a library of photos to chose from, you can take one using your computer's camera or the one in your **mobile phone** (see p.172).

Change the layout of your photos by dragging them above or below one another in the upload list.

Publishing posts ✓

Don't feel that you must immediately publish every new post you write. Using the sidebar that accompanies each post, you can set your post to go live at any future date, or save it as a **draft** and return to it later. Click the drop-down field that reads "publish now" to see those choices, plus options for adding the post to your ready-made **queue**, or making it private (private posts require your password to read). Do note – you can use simple descriptions like "tomorrow" to set the timing of future posts, but if you want to be very precise follow the mm/dd/yy 12:34am construction.

The queue

On your tumblr's control page you'll find a link to your queue, behind which can sit up to 300 posts, waiting to be released upon a schedule you set. You can rearrange the order of the posts by clicking and dragging them into place, dip back in to edit them before they go live, or publish them immediately. It's a nice option to have when trying to maintain a steady stream of fresh material.

From the sidebar you can add tags, **include sources**, set a custom URL or allow images within replies.

Quotes

You don't always have to let people know what's going on inside your head – often someone has already said what you're thinking, only better. If you come across some words of wisdom you want to share, click the **quote** icon in the blogging panel and paste in the quote along with an attribution and description.

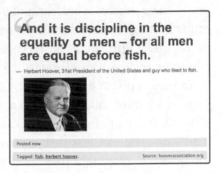

And it is discipline in the equality of men – for all men are equal before fish.

— Herbert Hoover, 31st President of the United States and guy who liked to fish.

Posted now

Tagged: fish, herbert hoover.

Source: hooverassociation.org

You can embed images within your quote descriptions, just like with your text posts.

Links and chats

Posting a **link** is the ultimate form of microblogging – you don't even have to provide a description (though people following you may like hearing your thoughts on the matter). Simply copy the URL from the article or image you want to share, paste it in place and it will appear as a link on your tumblr feed.

Chats are nearly as easy, though may require you to do a little reformatting so they read correctly. Get started by copying any **instant messaging** conversation, then pasting it into the chat posting option on your tumblr. Use a line break to differentiate between the parties, and your text will be displayed in alternating shaded and unshaded rows.

Audio posts

Especially useful for musicians, Tumblr lets you post one audio file per day from one of three sources: your computer, a music hosting site called **SoundCloud** or by direct link to a file accessible  anywhere on the web. Though it may seem like it should be more complicated than posting other sorts of content to your site, Tumblr makes it very easy to upload audio – they only ask that you officially hold the rights to share that file. And while you can just throw your file up on your tumblr for anyone to play right there on the page, you may want to take the time to add a description and include album cover artwork (www.albumart.org is a good source).

Video

If you're comfortable uploading photos (see p.159) you're sure to feel at ease with videos too. You can either add your own movies straight from your computer (as long as they're under ten minutes long and less than 100MB in size), or grab a link to a video online and share it through your tumblr. For the latter option, simply attach the link to the page with the video that you like, and it will appear as a post.

For additional display options, including the choice of resizing the video, find the **embed** button on the site where your video lives, and copy the code that appears behind it.

Multiple tumblrs

When you sign up for a Tumblr account, you'll be creating your primary tumblr at the same time. But you're not limited to that one blog – you can make as many tumblrs as you'd like and access them all from the same dashboard.

| trunchfiddle |
| CultFootball on tumbl |
| RGtoSocialMedia |
| Charles Johnson for... |
| Eggblogg |
| Create a new blog |

To create a new tumblr, find the "plus" icon at the top of your dashboard and click it. Then give your new tumblr a name and URL, and choose whether you want to **password protect** your posts (something you can't do with your primary tumblr). You don't have to choose protection right away – simply click the link to your added blog's settings and you'll see the option to password protect it at the very bottom of the page.

Only the first two blogs in your list are displayed along the top of your dashboard. Rearrange the order by dragging them into place.

Additional blogs also let you include **multiple contributors**. These people can post to your blog, and even adjust the page appearance if you grant them administrative privileges. Just click the **members** button on your blog's sidebar to invite contributors by email. To differentiate between contributors on your shared blogs, turn on **show author portraits**, found in the settings where you'd upload a new avatar (see p.155). Now whenever someone publishes a new post, his or her own avatar will accompany it.

Become a follower

Tumblr isn't just about voicing your own opinions and sharing your latest photos. It's also a great place to stay connected with what's happening in your community and around the world. And while it's nice to see your own thoughts up on the screen, your dashboard will be pretty bare until you start to **follow** a few other tumblrs. Let's take a look at some ways you can uncover tumblrs that may interest you, and discuss what to do about it when you find one.

The search

Finding new posts in tumblr is all about the **tags**. From your dashboard, look to the side panel where you'll find a search field, in which you can type any term or phrase. Tumblr will search through tags on every post, then scan all text content for your search terms before returning a dashboard's worth of results. If you think you might revisit your search terms with some frequency, you may want to **save** your search – just click the **track** button next to your highlighted term and it will stay in your sidebar from now on.

Search for a trending term, and options for refining results by **featured** and **popular** tags will appear – tracking will save them **all**.

The fields in Tumblr's explore tags **slideshow** arranges popular tags within an attention-grabbing display. It also searches popular users' **descriptions** for key terms to help categorize the results.

Above the search field will be an option to **explore tags**. Whereas search is wide open, Tumblr's exploring feature is much more focused. Click the link and you'll be taken to a panel of shifting images representing the hottest topics across Tumblr. Below that are columns of tags ranked by activity and feedback (you can reorder the content in these columns by clicking their headings). You'll also see the **top editor** associated with that tag – perhaps it's someone whose tumblr you might want to check out. Clicking any of the images or tags will bring you back to your dashboard, where you can scroll through page upon page of posts associated with that tag.

> **TIP:** Adding **tags** to your posts will help other people find you more easily and can help you search your own posts more effectively (click the arrow in the search box to focus your search on your own posts, or on other people's posts currently in your dashboard). Tags are especially useful when posting photo sets or videos without descriptive text.

What's in a blog?

People seem to have versions of themselves for different social media venues. Maybe you're chatty and jokey on Twitter but more sensitive on Google+. You're eager and accomplished on LinkedIn, while your Facebook profile may attest to your never-ending battles with various workplace miseries. Of all the major services, Tumblr is by far the most customizable; it also lets you fracture your **interests** across any number of blogs (see p.163) or stick with one particular theme that showcases a skill or talent.

Due in no small part to its flexibility, Tumblr has given rise to a number of beautifully **quirky** blogs. Tumblrs like www.scanwiches.com (where sandwiches are sliced in half and scanned, then presented next to an ingredients list) and www.kimjongillookingatthings.tumblr.com (in which the late Dear Leader stands looking at things) reveal their creators playful and artistic sides. Others can be **personal**, giving us a view into the daily struggles of an individual, such as Los Angeles designer Heather (www.hrrrthrrr.com). Still more exist solely to aggregate news stories that might otherwise go unnoticed, as with Anthony DeeRosa's www.soupsoup.tumblr.com. There are no rules about what to put in your tumblr, but whatever you choose make sure it comes from the heart.

Looking at a stereo system

166

Following

When starting out with a new tumblr, you will see the latest posts from the official Tumblr blog in your **dashboard**. Named "staff", this account will send you updates about the Tumblr service and highlight interesting blogs you

may want to check out. If something in the staff feed catches your eye, or if you find someone (or some company) using the search features described on p.164, you can follow that person so their posts show up on your dashboard too. Simply navigate to the page you want to follow (if you aren't already there) and click the **follow** button in the upper right-hand corner.

Tumblrs you follow will be collected behind the green **following** link found in your dashboard's sidebar. Click it and you'll see a list of everyone you follow, along with the option of **unfollowing** them. Be careful when you unfollow someone or something – you won't be given a prompt to confirm your intent, it will just be deleted. Here, you'll also find an option to **block** a tumblr, and after that you can report it for spam or harassment. Revisit that same block page if you ever want to lift the ban.

Your following page also lets you search for people in your Yahoo! or Hotmail

As you scroll through a page, quickly reset the view by clicking the **return to top** icon that will appear in the upper right corner of your screen.

address books or by AOL and MSN instant messenger handle. Like all the other services willing to match you up with your friends via **address book**, you'll need to give over your username and password, and trust that they won't use the information for evil. Similar to the "explore tags" feature accessible through your dashboard, your following page also contains a link to a browsing feature called **spotlight**. Here you can select a subject field from the list provided, and you'll be shown a selection of unique and original tumblrs as chosen by Tumblr.

> **TIP:** The spotlight is populated using secret algorithms only Tumblr knows, but if you feel your offerings deserve to be highlighted, you can drop them a note at: editors@tumblr.com.

I heart u

As you wander through posts both random and collected, you'll have the chance to **like** them. When reading a post on your dashboard, you'll see a dark little heart at its top. Click it and it will turn bright red as an indication of your approval. When roaming the odd tumblr, the liking process is a tad more involved. You'll need to open the post into its own page (accomplished by clicking either the **notes** or **likes** link found either below or to the side of each post), and from there, find the empty heart button in the upper right corner of the page to click it.

Back on your dashboard, you'll see a link to your liked posts in your sidebar. Click it and the page will change to one displaying all the posts you've given a heart, in chronological order. You won't be able to sort them any other way, but your collected likes can still serve as a **bookmarking** tool (see p.264), helping you find particular posts you want to revisit. Though, if you use your likes in this fashion, you'll want to **unlike** any posts that have

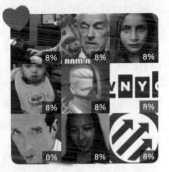

Tumblr crushes show the people whose posts you most frequently reblog or like. Once you hit a minimum of nine likes or follows, you'll find this box displayed on your following page.

served their purpose (by clicking the red heart and turning it a still grey); otherwise, your collection will become too unwieldy to be of much use.

Reblogging

When you stumble across a great post on Tumblr, don't keep it to yourself – **reblog** it so that the people following you can share in the experience. Posts listed in your dashboard will have a reblog link right along the top. For posts out in the

wild, open the full view for that post and look in the top right corner of the page for the reblog button. Select it, and you'll open a page that looks very much like the one you'd see if you were creating a new post (see p.158). The only difference here is the choice of changing the current **style** of post. For instance, instead of reblogging a photo in its current form, you can **change** it to a text, link or quote post but clicking the **as** button at its top. As you change the style of the post, the blogging options will adjust to suit.

Attracting attention

As with Twitter and Google+, no one you follow on Tumblr is required to follow you back. But with all the great content you're sure to share, it'd be a shame if no one was around to see it. So how exactly do you increase your numbers?

Well, there's nothing "exact" about it unfortunately. While you can buy followers or join services like www.tumbletrain .com to get a quick boost, what's most attractive to potential followers is a well-designed page (see p.152), top-notch content and pictures, pictures, pictures! Earning **likes** and **reblogs** will expose you to more followers, and pictures tend to draw nearly three times the reblogs as plain text posts.

You'll also want to make sure you have a clever or attractive avatar (see p.155), along with a memorable tumblr title that conveys a sense of the material behind it. If you have accounts with **Facebook** and **Twitter**, post a link to your tumblr whenever you write a new post. Make comments on other people's tumblrs so they'll be inclined to visit yours, and don't be ashamed to ask people to follow you in exchange for following them – it's a common practice.

Preferences

Settings handle how each of your tumblr blogs behave at an individual level, but to control your dashboard and overall account, you'll need to dip into your preferences. Here you'll be able to change your **password**, hide your likes from visitors and manage email alerts. Click the **gear** icon in the control strip at the top of your page to begin.

Edit, display, notify

Beneath the options for changing your primary **email address** and password, you're given the choice of how you'd like to edit your posts. The web savvy might try HTML or Markdown as a default, though the rest of us should stick with rich text. Next, you'll see options for showing full-size **photos** (instead of the expandable thumbnails currently displayed in your dashboard posts), controlling how often the little alert will pop up indicating new posts, combining all your inboxes and allowing posts to endlessly slide under one another as you scroll down the page. You'll also see settings keyed to actions that tumblr should **email** you about. Your multiple blogs have individual settings, so you can receive an email if someone joins, messages or reblogs from one, while keeping a muzzle on another.

If you choose to **delete** your account (click the link at the bottom of your preferences), Tumblrbot will be sad to see you go.

Mobile

Just about anything you can do in the web version of Tumblr can be accomplished right from your **smartphone**, and even "dumb" phones have some access (as long as they can send email, see p.174). Head to your respective smartphone's app store to download the free software, and sign in with your regular account information to get started.

Dashboard to go

As in the web version, upon opening the mobile app you'll be taken to your dashboard and a list of all the most recent posts from the tumblrs you follow. You can reblog or like them as normal, and expand the **notes** to see who else has been liking and reblogging them. Tap any tumblr name to

see choices for reading all current posts, or if you've become tired of someone, you can **unfollow** with a tap of the minus sign. You'll also have the option of browsing through their likes – if they've enabled that option in their preferences (see p.171).

Multiple photos in posts are indicated by a series of circles at the bottom of the picture. Swipe left or right to scroll through them.

Posting

Posting in the Tumblr app is very similar to (if not quite as nuanced as) posting in its web cousin. Tap the **post** button and you'll see all your blogs listed along the bottom. Slide them right or left until the one you want to post from is centered under the posting options. Now click the type of post you want to create and fill the subsequent screen with your words and pictures.

> **TIP:** To edit or **delete** one of your posts, either head to the dashboard and locate the post there, or fine tune your search using the posts option under blog control.

There are some differences you're sure to notice. For one, you won't be able to upload any music saved on your phone into an **audio** post (you'll have to record a live note using your phone's microphone). There's also no front-and-centre icon to post a chat (it's under quotes, and called "dialogue" now).

But you will be able to take **pictures** and **video** right from the app and immediately upload them inside a post. It's even possible to

While avatars are visible for your individual and group tumblrs, private tumblrs show only a padlock icon.

Tumblr by email

We can't always rely on access to a computer, and not all of us have the latest smartphones. If you find yourself with nothing but the email option on your "dumb" phone and you're desperate to post, you can send an email to the secret address provided in your tumblr's **settings** (see p.155) to create a new post of any type.

You won't have all the fancy buttons that help guide the style and formatting of your posts online, but that won't stop you from differentiating between a text and a photo post – or any other kind for that matter. The subject line of your email will become its title, and if your message starts with text it will default to a **text** post. Adding a photo first, with text underneath, creates a **photo** post with description, while embedding multiple photos will display a photoset – **audio** and **video** posts work the same way. Wrap your email in quotations, add a dash and a name, and it will become a **quote** with accompanying attribution. To create a **link** post, simply copy in the URL; and for **chats**, set it up as you would if organizing the exchange using Tumblr's web version (see p.161). Finally, using **tags** in any post is done similarly to tagging something in Twitter (see p.126). Simply throw a hashmark in front of any #word at the bottom of your email, and it will end up in your tagged terms.

tag posts, save them as drafts, send them to your queue (see p.160), or create a permalink of your own design. To accomplish this, open a new post and you'll see miniature **circle** and **gear** icons at the bottom of the screen. Slide your finger to the left (engaging the gear) to open a page of these options, plus the choice of switching which of your multiple blogs should be the author of the post. Slide your finger back to the right to keep editing your post.

> **TIP:** We mentioned earlier that collecting your likes in one page is a sort of makeshift **bookmarking** service (see p.264). In the mobile app this finds its best use, as the posts you want to share face-to-face are now as close as the touch of the **like** button.

Blog control

Clicking the blog icon at the bottom of the screen reveals a sideways scrolling list of your multiple blogs, similar to what you saw behind the post button – but here you'll have the choice of browsing through your posts and followers, answering **messages**, and managing posts in your

Tap **answer** to reply to queries in your message box (or remove it with the "×"). Be warned – your reply will be posted to your blog.

175

drafts and queue. You also have the option of customizing your tumblr, though this won't give you access to the design features available in the web version (see p.152). Here, you'll only be able to change your tumblr's name and adjust its **description**.

Following accounts

Tumblr isn't shy about suggesting blogs you might enjoy, and you shouldn't be wary of trying a few out (you can always delete them, see p.167). If you allow Tumblr access to your email or instant message address books, they can help you find friends' tumblrs (see p.168). They'll offer to scan your phone's **contacts** to find matches, and encourage you to add some recommended blogs based on your previous choices.

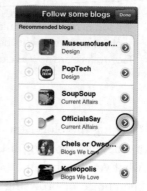

Tap the **arrow** to check out a tumblr's latest posts before committing to following it.

LinkedIn

Get to work

Of all the social media networks out there, LinkedIn is the only one that exists specifically to help advance your career. Members, of whom the majority operate within the corporate world, use the site to make and manage connections based on professional relationships, as opposed to the personal relationships that are at the core of Facebook.

A LinkedIn profile page consists almost entirely of academic and professional accomplishments. Your profile becomes your living résumé, which you can update at any time and enhance with links to portfolios and recommendations. LinkedIn makes it simple to identify and apply for new jobs, and also allows recruiters to scan your experience and determine if you might be a match for an open position. But, as anyone who's looked for a job will know, there's more to getting hired than your experience – it takes good timing, a helpful hand and a bit of luck. LinkedIn helps you stay in touch with the changes in your industry, and to meet people at companies where you want to work – as for the luck, you're on your own.

Getting started

To sign up for an account, visit www.linkedin.com and fill in your name, email address, and password (see p.28 for tips on creating strong **passwords**). You'll be asked if you're currently employed, still a student or looking to hire someone new at your company  – though the majority of us will use LinkedIn to promote ourselves and our work, keep in mind that there's someone watching from the other side. Take the time to provide your location and, depending on your status, your current company, industry or academic institution. These fields are the first step in creating a strong, professional **network**. If you can't fill them out now, or any information changes over time, be sure to head to your **profile** to make the adjustments (see p.184) before contacting people and sending out **job applications** (see p.200).

Search your addresses

It would be unusual if a social media service *didn't* want to search your email address book for potential connections already using their service. You have the choice of ignoring the request, though it is one of the best ways to branch out quickly. Unlike on Facebook and other sites, where you may want to keep your identity hidden from employers and colleagues, here you very much want to make yourself visible – your professional self, that is. There's likely to be some crossover between your personal and professional social media accounts, but in LinkedIn the focus is strictly on the work.

> **TIP:** You can search for email addresses at any time using the **add connections** option found under the **contacts** button (see p.191).

Paid or free?

Before further developing your profile, there is the matter of choosing a **plan**. Basic accounts are free, and allow members to create profiles, build networks through personal, professional and academic connections, and search and apply for jobs. Paying for **premium** service enables features such as seeing who visited your profile page, contacting users who are not direct connections (see p.191), making additional **introductions** (see p.195) and being pushed to the top of the pile when applying for a job (see p.200). The services available at the basic level are considerable, and

Advanced search features can help narrow the focus to a particular field, job level or salary history, but only come as part of a premium business or recruiter account. These business-side accounts also enable automated searches that will alert you when a candidate meets your requirements.

What's in it for me?

For anyone on a job hunt, a LinkedIn profile is almost a prerequisite for candidacy. As companies increasingly reference social media profiles during the evaluation period, making LinkedIn your primary (or only) **public** social media profile is effective – if not downright critical – in managing both your reputation and professional record. Even if you aren't currently looking for a job, maintaining an accurate, up-to-date presence on LinkedIn is great for **networking**. Making yourself available for enquiries or introductions from people interested in your expertise is never a bad thing.

Just because LinkedIn is a social media site for professionals does not mean your profile page has to be stale, however. Highlight your **skills** and **accomplishments** (you speak three languages!), or put a spotlight on interesting projects you've developed (you created a website that catalogues slang in those languages!). Listing these on your member profile will help to distinguish you and your work from the millions of other LinkedIn users.

should be sufficient for most members. But those of us on the job hunt may appreciate the ability to reach out and promote ourselves a little more aggressively. If you don't opt into a premium level at sign-up, you can always **upgrade** (check under your **more** tab for paid options).

Bring your work home

The centre of your LinkedIn experience is your **home** page. Here you'll see a mixture of account alerts, news headlines (see p.204) and updates from everyone you're connected to. Click the **more** button at the top of the feed and you'll be able to narrow the view to newly updated profiles, photos and jobs, or to limit it to new posts from companies and groups (see p.197). You may also see the occasional **tweet** in your feed – if a contact has connected their Twitter and LinkedIn accounts (see p.190). You can post your own updates, and share links to pictures and articles on the web, using the **share an update** box at the top of the page.

As you scroll through updates from recruiters and absorb who's now connected to whom, you'll have the chance to like, comment upon and share what you're reading. If an update originated on Twitter (indicated by "via Twitter" next to the member's name), you can save it as a favourite, **retweet** it or reply to it as you can with any regular tweet (see p.137).

Companies You May Want To Follow

CRC PRESS

CAMBRIDGE UNIVERSITY PRESS

hachette

Sandvik enriching young minds

Barefoot Books

EMC Publishing

Feedback | See more »

The right side of your home page is populated with a series of links to people you may know, activity alerts, jobs that match your skill set, and groups and companies in which you may be interested. You'll also see a button to add a live link to your blog at the very bottom (see p.190).

Portrait of a professional

The key to attracting the right sort of attention is having an accurate and fully developed profile. To begin, move your mouse over the **profile** button on the navigation toolbar and select **edit** from the drop-down menu. You'll be taken to your profile page, which at first will be pretty bare. Fortunately, LinkedIn has provided numerous ways to help you add and organize information about yourself, and even lets you point to outside examples of your work using third-party applications (see p.190).

Add a résumé

When starting with a new profile you'll be doing a lot of clicking and typing to input all of your information. Alternatively, sidestep the tedium of data entry by **uploading** your résumé. In order for it to be readable by LinkedIn, you'll need to have the file saved in a Word (ending with .doc or .docx), PDF, text or HTML format not exceeding 500KB in size. Click the **import your résumé** link, found in the blue-hued box on the right side of your screen, choose

Click any heading along the **navigation bar** at the top of your screen to reveal a list of related options and actions.

the file from your computer's hard drive and send it to LinkedIn. Be warned, résumé-upload software is inaccurate at best – any sort of odd formatting in your original document will produce some strange results. Be sure you follow their prompts to **review** and verify the automated output so that everything appears in the correct fields. You can also completely remove any imported position before saving these changes to your profile. If for some reason the résumé import didn't work properly, you can simply return to the editing page without saving by clicking **go back** at the bottom of the review page.

> **TIP:** Click **view profile** to see what your profile looks like to other people. Links here let you email your profile to other people, save it as a PDF or send a copy straight to your printer.

Hands-on experience

Adjusting and adding fields one at a time may not be as quick as the automated import, but the option always exists. Simply click **edit** by any current field or look for the tiny plus sign to add new **sections** and experiences. Rather than plainly list all of your positions along with information about where the company is located and what position you held there, you'll want to take

To Do:
- Update your experience
- Update your education
- Add your skills

12x more career opportunities

time to provide a brief **description** of what you did (or still do). Be as general or as specific as you wish, though it may be in your best interest to provide as much detail as possible. What kind of meaningful tasks do you perform? Do you oversee a team? Have you consistently operated on budget? These can take the form of a bulleted list or a short paragraph – either way, giving people a sense of what you do will help create better matches to open positions and with other people in your industry. As you continue to add to and edit your profile, a bar on the right side of the page will track your progress towards completion.

LinkedIn provides a constant reminder of which fields you're missing in the profile completeness panel. Tap any **plus sign** to fill out that part of your LinkedIn profile.

Summarize it

People visiting your profile are greeted with a snapshot of your accomplishments, below which sits a prose **summary** of your experience and goals. It's not mandatory to fill in this field, but as on most of LinkedIn, it really is a good idea. Your profile page has to **stand out** in searches and survive being skimmed – a hiring manager or headhunter may not have the time or the inclination to scroll through the rest of your page if your summary isn't moving. And while it seems impossible that such a unique talent as yours could be adequately described so briefly, it is in your best interest to have a summary that is succinct, readable and **attention-grabbing**. It's worth spending whatever time is necessary getting two or three sentences just right if it means your entire profile gets a proper look.

> **TIP:** If you would like to post your résumé in any number of **other languages**, look for the "create your profile in another language" link toward the upper right of your edit profile page. You can switch between language profiles using the drop-down link found just above the "improve your profile" button.

Add a picture

Just like any other social network, a profile picture helps convey a sense of who you are. But unlike other networks, you won't get the chance to pluck a new profile photo from among your many albums and tagged photos (see p.65) – here you only get one. And while it may be fun to upload a picture of a cute animal as your Twitter **avatar** (see p.120), your LinkedIn picture should actually be you. If you want colleagues and potential employers to take you seriously, make sure you use a photograph showing your best side. It's easy to judge a book by its cover – consider your photo the cover to your profile.

Prepare for contact

LinkedIn is all about contact. Once your profile is established, most of your time on LinkedIn should be spent reaching out to other people or responding to **requests** and messages. We'll address contacting other people later in the chapter (see p.191). For now, let's take a look at letting people know what sort of enquiries you're willing to entertain.

Specific to premium versions of LinkedIn, **InMail** allows you to email anyone within the system, even if you aren't yet connected.

Close to the bottom of your profile page you'll see a link to "change contact preferences", behind which are a series of options that will hopefully help reduce **inbox** overload. By default, you'll be signed up to hear from everyone about everything. But you may only be interested in hearing about **new ventures**, not enquiries into open positions at your company. Tick the boxes that correspond with the type of opportunities you want to know about, and fill in the **advice** field with precise information on what kinds of projects you'd consider.

Before saving your changes, take a moment to think about exactly who you want contacting you. If you only accept **introductions** (see p.195), you will only hear from your contacts. But if you grant access for both introductions and InMail, you'll hear from anyone (including headhunters and recruiters) willing to pay for premium service.

Rounding out your résumé

Once you leap the hurdle of immodesty, you're sure to have more to say about yourself than might fit within LinkedIn's major headings. Still, there are valuable parts of your history and personality that potential employers and business colleagues may find interesting, or see as a point of commonality. Perhaps you want to highlight your performance background with your university a cappella group, or prove your writing chops with the blog you keep – but you wouldn't exactly call either one professional experience. LinkedIn realizes this, and has created space where you can exhibit selections from your unique background.

When viewing your education details, select **add** a school, or **edit** one listed already, to see fields for activities, societies and additional notes. Belonging to an alumni club has helped more than one person get ahead in this world, so be sure to include that along with any notes about your stellar academic or extracurricular endeavours.

Back in your overall profile, you'll see a field for **additional information**. Use this area to link to your websites or blogs, provide some of your interests as **talking points** during interviews and highlight any honours or awards you received while working in your professional roles. You'll also see the **groups** and associations you've joined through LinkedIn, along with the option of hiding any one of them from prying eyes.

189

Applications

Besides being a place to promote yourself and develop connections, LinkedIn can be used as a hub for group collaboration. On your profile, click **add an application** at the bottom of the page and you'll see a number of apps intended to help you share information across your network. You can use them to help promote the things you've done personally, or inform groups and organizations with whom you're connected of articles, research and results you may all find relevant.

Share your tweets with LinkedIn's Twitter client, found on the applications page. You can choose to share updates in one or both directions.

Perhaps a recruiter wants to see some examples of your work, or your team is putting the finishing touches to a big presentation – productivity applications like **Box.net Files** or **Google Presentations** could service both needs. For lighter interactions, consider exchanging book recommendations using Amazon's Reading List, or keep your connections in the loop with updates from your WordPress blog (see p.144).

> **TIP:** Click **add sections** while editing your profile page to highlight projects, publications, volunteer work, fluency in additional languages and any relevant awards or certifications. You can click and drag any profile field to **rearrange** their order.

Get connected

Now that you've filled in all your profile fields and are satisfied with your work, it's time to sit back, put your feet up and wait for the offers to come rolling in, right? *Wrong*. It's crucial to **reach out** and meet new contacts in your chosen profession, and just as important to stay in touch with people you've worked with over the years. LinkedIn can help with both.

Work and school

You had the chance to start populating your network at the start, when LinkedIn asked to look through your email address books (see p.180). Click **contacts** on the navigation bar followed by **add connections** and you'll see that same option. Along the top of this page are tabs with choices for searching out **colleagues** and **alumni**, based on the information you recorded in the experience and education portions of your profile. Choosing the former opens a list of all your listed companies – click any to reveal all the people currently employed there. You'll be allowed to choose names, and group them into what will become a

Adding a message to a connection request isn't mandatory, but it certainly is recommended.

mass invite. But even here you have the option of including a personal message, and while "personal" and "group" do seem terms at odds, you can still add a few words to remind people of why they, on the whole, matter to you.

Combing through your old school chums is a more refined affair. Click a school button on the **alumni** tab and you'll see a page displaying thumbnails of classmates who attended at the same time as you. Chances are you'll have some connection between you already, so most of your class should be only as far as one **degree** away (see overleaf). You can search a different date range using the drop-down buttons at the top of the page, or search for a specific person using the "search for alumni profiles" option. At the very bottom, after the option to expand findings past the first dozen or so, you'll see an ad to join your alumni **group** (see p.189).

Your school: University of Chicago ▾			
Where they work...		**What they do...**	
Motorola Mobility	188	Finance	2214
University of Illinois at Chicago	182	Information technology	1996
University of Chicago	165	Entrepreneur	1914
Chicago Public Schools	165	Administrative	1838
Accenture	129	Medical	1782
show more...		show more...	

Your alumni network has the potential to become very strong, and LinkedIn helpfully generates **statistics** to show who among your old study partners is closest to you in profession and location. Clicking any field will take you to a search page listing all the people falling under that designation.

You're invited

Whenever you send out an invitation to connect, the recipient will receive a message in their LinkedIn **inbox** along with an email alert -- assuming they haven't changed their default email settings (see p.203). From the inbox, they can accept your invitation or choose to ignore it. Hopefully they accept, after which you'll be immediately added to each other's networks. Not only is it beneficial to be directly in touch with people you know, but as you expand your **first degree connections**, you'll be opening yourself up to second- and third-level connections, making it possible to reach out to, and be reached, by more and more people without having to pay for premium service (see p.181).

People can reply to your invitations before accepting them, in which case you'll see an alert in your own inbox (along with any invitations coming your way). If your invitation didn't include a few lines about who you are and why your shared history suggests a connection, they may simply not remember you and ignore it. If given the chance to explain yourself, be sure to send the message you should've included in your initial request.

How closely you're connected to other LinkedIn users is indicated by a tiny **degree** icon next to their name. Degrees limit direct messaging past the first level, and are a primary component of **introductions** – a referral system used within the site (see p.195).

General searches

Not everyone worth connecting with will have been a classmate or someone you've worked alongside. You can always search for any number of people, companies and **jobs** (see p.200) using the search box at the top of every page, but a better way is by clicking advanced search, then choosing **find people**. Here you'll see an extensive list of options that will limit your search to locations, industries, schools and languages. You'll even be able to focus on specific levels of connection, so you don't waste your time sorting through a bunch of strangers you've never met. At first you'll see options based upon your current connections, previous employment and schooling, but you can search for any person, place or thing using individual search boxes in each field.

TIP: Found under contacts in your navigation bar, **network statistics** collects information about where your contacts live and what they do. Choose any breakdown and you'll be brought to the standard search page, with the boxes generating those results selected. You can refine your search manually from there.

Introductions

LinkedIn will let you send a connection request to anyone on the site, but if that person doesn't know you, chances are you'll be shot down. When it comes to contacting a member with whom you are not personally acquainted, check your network to see if you know

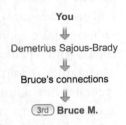

someone in common who might be able to **introduce** you to each other. First, click the person's name and navigate to their full profile. Then choose the "get introduced through a connection" link on the right-hand side of the page. Select your common connection and add a message explaining why it's worth joining each other's networks. Once you send your request, your current connection will have the choice of passing it along, or shutting you out.

Joining groups

Shared interests, such as a love of gardening, can help you meet new friends on sites like Facebook (see p.53), but on LinkedIn groups are strictly for developing connections across your industry. Hover your mouse over the **groups** link in your navigation toolbar to reveal options for managing, finding and **creating** groups. Before tackling that last option, you might

Any pending actions regarding your account (including group requests) will be highlighted with an info button.

try browsing through groups you may like, or searching the **groups directory** by keyword, type and language.

Many groups are open, meaning you can join immediately. Others require approval for membership – those appear with a padlock icon next to their name. Attempting to join a closed group sends a request to its administrator, who will then approve or deny your request. Your entry ticket will sit under the **your groups** link while awaiting the okay. Here, you can choose to send a message to the administrator explaining why you'd like to be included in their clique. Alternatively, you may **withdraw** your request and it will disappear as if it never were.

> **TIP:** Some discussions are clearly spam. Flag them as inappropriate using the **more** drop-down menu under any post.

Once you're part of a group, you can check in on discussions, browse its members, see who is promoting new work or search through related job posts. Of all the options, **discussions** are the most visible, and will be the most likely to spark interactions with people you haven't previously encountered. Starting a popular discussion thread and remaining engaged can solidify your reputation as an expert (or at least a reliable source) in industry networks. Voices of experience and reason tend to draw followers – just be sure you don't overreach. It's better to keep quiet and have people think you're a fool, than open your mouth and prove it.

Creating a group

Though many of us will find our niche represented by an existing group, there's always room for another. Starting your own **group** is a relatively straightforward affair. Simply give it a name and description, indicate its type and location, and choose whether you'll accept anyone or if you want the right of refusal. You'll also have the option of uploading a **logo** and linking a Twitter account to the group (it's a good idea to have a dedicated Twitter account for your LinkedIn group rather than using a personal one). Add the email domain of people you'll grant immediate access, eg @roughguides .com, and your group is ready for the world.

Professional etiquette

While social media is a fairly new way of engaging and communicating with other people, the rules that apply to networking in person still apply. "Please" and "thank you" help create a positive impression in social media, just as they do in the real world. Good manners are never old-fashioned, nor should they be. This is especially important when it comes to making professional connections and searching for work. Your hard work and immaculate résumé could be undone by typo-ridden emails or the failure to send a thank you note after an interview. If you are unsure as to how to use LinkedIn appropriately, the **answers** feature under the **more** menu, where members ask and answer questions using their own expertise, should be a big help.

Get recommended

A good word can push your résumé to the top of the pile. LinkedIn understands this, and has developed an unique system that will share praise you've received with people viewing your profile. Part traditional **endorsement**, part customer service record, LinkedIn recommendations can help get your profile seen by more users, as well as testify to the **quality** of your work and the truth of your experience.

Asking nicely

When you select **recommendations** (found under the profile tab in your navigation bar) you'll see tabs to help you manage your received, requested and sent recommendations. While anyone is able to recommend the people they've worked with, it's much more likely you'll need to reach out and ask. Under **requests**, choose the position your colleagues or customers will know you from, then fill in the names of all the people whose kind words you seek. If you're requesting a recommendation from a former colleague who is also a former classmate, selecting the appropriate experience

Sent recommendations can be displayed on your profile page. Choose wisely, you don't want someone's poor work tarnishing your own.

Sean Recommends (2) edit

Lash LaRue, *person, Place*
    Lash is a great worker.

Joseph (Seph) Petta, *Writer/Editor, Rough Guides Travel Publisher*
    Joesph is a fine author and editor who is both...

Manage **Recommendations** »

here will make sure that the recommendation is accurately tailored to your profile.

Sharing like for like

It's not uncommon to offer a recommendation in **exchange** for someone sending one back, and it's simple enough to initiate the interaction. Make your way to the **sent** portion of the screen and you'll have the choice of endorsing colleagues, service providers, business partners and any student with whom you may have studied or taught (there are also controls for choosing which of your sent recommendations you'd like displayed on your profile page). You'll have the chance to explain your position in relation to that person, and define what companies or schools you were associated with at the time. Add in your thoughtful public letter of

recommendation, then attach a private note that mentions how you're trying to build up your own LinkedIn profile, and would appreciate them returning the favour. You can always **withdraw** the recommendation if it doesn't work out.

Find a job

Now that you've gotten in touch with old classmates and colleagues, and maybe even made some new connections along the way, it's time to start using that network to advance your career. Staying in touch with your contacts may be the best way to hear about open positions, but you'd be doing yourself a disservice if you waited for something to fall into your lap. LinkedIn has you covered, with job search tools that are simple to use alongside helpful application support.

Check the listings

Start your search under the **jobs** link in your navigation bar. You can return manual results by job title, keyword or company name, or use the advanced search to filter jobs by industry, location, level of experience or how recently the post went live. Alternatively, check LinkedIn's suggestions – they've combed your profile to match open positions with the information you provided.

Click the title of any job posting to access its full description. If it looks like a good fit, you can **apply** for it with the push of a button – doing so will open an application form asking for your résumé and cover letter. Along with these, LinkedIn will send a copy of your profile to the potential employer. If you're not quite ready to apply, **save** the job and return to it later under the **saved jobs** tab. You can also **share** a job with someone if you think they'd be interested using LinkedIn's mail system, Facebook or Twitter.

TIP: Save your keyword searches and have the results emailed to you on a daily, weekly or monthly basis. You can access and edit saved searches from your jobs page.

Companies

Getting to know a company before you apply is key to explaining why you'd make the perfect employee in your cover letter. Many companies have profiles on LinkedIn, where they post updates about events and product releases alongside calls for applications. The company profile page can also show you who in your network already works there, and might be able to get you an **introduction** to someone else at the company who's hiring.

Once you decide to **follow** a company, you can check back in on them at any time under the **following** tab on your jobs page. You're also able to set daily or weekly alerts so you'll be notified when people in that company leave or are promoted, or if new jobs are posted in their feed.

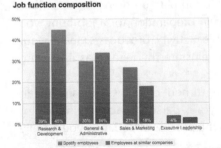

Job function composition

Use LinkedIn's **statistics** tools to discover the most popular positions at your favourite companies. You can also learn how quickly they've grown in the past few years, who their main competitors are and what kind of experience you need to work there.

Keeping it quiet

Searching for a job while unemployed is stressful, but at least you can be open about it. If you're working, but looking for something new, you'll want to promote yourself discreetly, maybe even in secret. LinkedIn is aware of your dilemma, and has installed various **privacy** settings that allow you to move about without revealing your identity or attracting unwanted attention.

Move the mouse over your name in the upper right-hand corner of any LinkedIn page, then click **settings** to reveal controls for everything from email preferences to account options like changing your email and password. Select profile to bring up your **privacy controls** and let's begin.

Walk softly

Whenever you make a change to your profile, you'll send out an **activity broadcast** that will be displayed on the home page of all your connections. Lots of activity updates give people the impression that you're getting ready to put yourself on the market. If you plan on doing some serious updating to your profile in preparation for a job hunt, you would do well to disable activity broadcasts, make your changes in secret, then reinstate the feature as if nothing ever happened.

Just because you've turned off alerts doesn't mean someone can't check your personal **activity feed** for changes. While you're in the process of updating your profile you should also set your activity feed visibility to **only you**. Even if you're not looking for a new job and just doing a bit of housekeeping this is still a good idea – no one wants to see something disorganized and half-complete. Alert people after you've finished the work.

Cover your tracks

You're able to keep your **profile picture** hidden and restrict who can see your **connections**, but anyone you're connected to will always be able to see your profile. That doesn't mean they need to see if you've been checking out theirs. Choose "what others see when you've viewed their profile", switch the choice to anonymous and you'll leave no trace behind.

To keep your identity secreted away from the greater Internet community, adjust your **public profile** so you'll be invisible to web searches – though that may stop you from hearing about some interesting opportunities. You may instead want to simply limit how much of your public profile strangers can see. Leaving just your basics open may be enough, though if you're comfortable with it you can reveal practically everything.

LinkedIn may have it's own messaging system, but it's hooked directly to your email – meaning you will hear about it every time a new alert comes in. Turn down the chatter by adjusting the settings in your email frequency.

News

Word spreads fast in today's 24-hour news cycle, and it's been sped up even more with the introduction of social media. Riots in Tottenham, an earthquake in Washington DC, the death of Osama bin Laden – people tapped into social media learned about these events almost instantly on their computers and mobiles, not from a broadcast or broadsheet.

LinkedIn Today, LinkedIn's news aggregator, won't focus on the latest headlines from politics and sports. Instead, it keeps you informed of all the most mentioned stories by people within your industry. Key to this structure is **sharing**, both from outside websites where you'll see a tiny "in" button next to articles (click it to post an update to your home page), and within LinkedIn itself (using the **share** button found below every article). You can **save** stories that are particularly interesting and return to them at any time, or choose to **follow** a particular news source, as recommended in a box on the right-hand side of any news page.

Trending articles get top placement and a brief description in the news section. Click the icon to see who among the community has publicly shared the piece.

Mobile

You never know when opportunity will knock, so it'd be terribly unfortunate if you weren't home when it came visiting. Luckily, LinkedIn has created a free smartphone app that will let you get in touch with your contacts and receive alerts wherever you may go.

Stay connected

Though not as robust as on the website version, the key elements of LinkedIn are accessible through the mobile app. You can share **updates** and browse your **groups**, search for people and check the news. And though you can't make adjustments to your experience, education and the rest, you can swap your profile pic – nice to have when you've just captured your best side with your mobile's camera.

Tap the **updates** icon and you'll be taken to a page topped with stories from LinkedIn Today, along with posts from connections (including Twitter rebroadcasts). Selecting any update lets you like, comment or **reshare** the post to your own profile. You can also send a post directly to one of your connections, or reply privately to the original author.

Click the "in" button to be brought back to your home page.

Addition in motion

Regardless of what you might think after reading this book, face-to-face meetings still happen. Your real world connections will almost always be stronger than the ones you maintain exclusively online, but that doesn't mean you shouldn't use LinkedIn's features to help you stay in touch with everyone you know.

While sitting on the train after a successful meeting with colleagues or customers, take a moment to click **groups & more** in the mobile app, and do a search for the people you've just met. You'll be able to connect with them right there from your phone – but you won't be able to send an accompanying note, so it really is best to strike while you're still fresh in their minds. You can also scroll through LinkedIn's suggested connections and add the people you know as you come across them.

Clicking someone's name will reveal their entire profile (excluding any web-based apps, see p.190). You can also check their recent activity, see who you have in common, pick through their list of connections, and email or **call** them directly (if they've published their phone number).

Google+

The new sheriff in town

Isn't it enough that the word "Google" is already synonymous with "look something up on the Internet" without their getting into social media too? Truth be told, Google has been in the social media business for longer than you may have realized, with services like YouTube, Picasa and Blogger at the front of their respective fields. Why shouldn't the undisputed champion of Internet search take a shot at Facebook and Twitter and their domination of social networking?

It's certainly worth the effort when the result is Google+. Where Facebook leans toward unwieldy, Google+ has a clean interface that is simple and intuitive to use. It takes the concept of following without being followed as introduced by Twitter, and seamlessly integrates other Google services such as Google Reader (see p.246), YouTube (see p.262) and Google search next to social features including chat, photo sharing and collaborative gaming. And while the network may initially nudge you to connect with certain users, there is no sustained pressure to reach out to old friends or rivals you'd have rather forgotten. Let's take a closer look at it all…

Sign me up

Before you're granted access to Google+, you'll need a **Google account**. If you use gmail (see p.22) or another Google service like Reader or Google Docs, you'll already have one. If none of this sounds familiar, direct your browser to http://accounts.google.com, where you'll be asked to provide a current email address, date of birth, location and a password of your choosing. In exchange, you'll be given access to the entire suite of Google services.

Google account in hand, proceed to http://plus.google.com and enter your account's username and password in the fields provided. Click submit and you'll see a black box asking you to update your public Google **Join** profile. Confirm your first name, last name and specify your gender. You can also upload your first **profile photo** at this time – if you don't have one on hand it's simple enough to add one later (see p.216). If you don't want Google using your **+1's** (which are the equivalent of Facebook's "likes", see p.230) to focus their advertising efforts on sites outside Google+, untick the box that reads "Google may use my information to personalize content and ads on non-Google web sites."

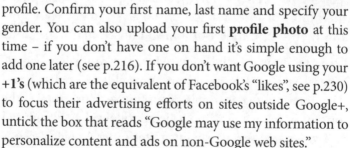

Whenever you visit any Google site while logged into your Google account, you'll see a black navigation panel across the top of your browser's page. Simply click a service (like your Google+ account) to be taken there instantly.

210

Tell us more

After clicking "join", Google+ will ask if you'd like to add people you know to **circles**. They'll also suggest you follow the posts of interesting and famous people who maintain Google+ profiles. Circles control everything you see and share on Google+. We'll discuss circles more fully a little later on (see p.218), but for now consider them as you would your real-life circles of friends. For instance, some people are very close to you, while others are simply acquaintances or work buddies. Same goes for family members, teammates, committees – if you can put a label on your relationship with a person, you can put them in a circle.

> **TIP:** Signing up for a **Google account** with a Yahoo! or Hotmail email address will elicit a prompt to connect those services to Google+ (and may require you to verify your account over the phone). Doing so will make it easier to find people in your Yahoo! or Hotmail address book who already use Google+.

Moving past your first experience with circles, Google+ will ask a few questions about where and when you went to school and where you work and live now. You'll also get another prompt to upload a profile photo. Putting a face to the name will help friends identify you more easily, but there's nothing stopping you from hiding behind a random shot. No worries if you're not ready, adjusting your profile photo is an option that never goes away (see p.216).

Make yourself at home

The first place you're always taken when visiting Google+ is your **home** screen. Before launching into creating posts (see p.222) and uploading your entire photo album (see p.237), let's take a second to get acquainted with your home's layout and features.

Everything in its place

Your home page is dominated by the **stream** – a listing of all the posts from friends and followers you've previously sorted into circles. The stream will also display your own posts, as well as the occasional "what's hot" alert shared by Google+ to everybody in the network.

> **TIP:** Check the entire **what's hot** feed at any time by clicking the flaming icon found by your saved searches on the left-hand side of the screen (see p.229).

Along the top of your page you'll see a **search** bar that will find any person or topic across the whole of Google+ – it would be strange if the king of Internet searches didn't provide such an option – and to the left of that is your **navigation panel**. Clicking any of these icons will take you to that specific portion of the site. Hover your mouse over any icon, and a pop-up hint will tell you where that icon leads.

Menus on either side of the stream help you navigate other social aspects of the Google+ experience. The left menu lists all of your circles, saved searches (see p.229) and games you've played most often (see p.244), and provides access to **Google Chat** – Google's instant messaging service. On the right, Google+ displays the profile photos of recently added and popular people in your circles. They also provide a quick link to invite more people by email (see p.217), as well as buttons to create a **hangout** (see p.234) or your own **Google+ page** (see p.241). At the very bottom there's a gentle nudge to waste some time with one of a few promoted games.

Click the Google+ logo at anytime, from any page, and you'll be taken to your home.

Video on demand

Google's ownership of **YouTube** has made it incredibly easy to search for videos and post them right to your page (for more on videos, see p.262). Click the floating YouTube logo along the right-hand side of your screen and a text prompt will appear. Typing in a word or phrase, or pasting in a URL then hitting enter, triggers a pop-up YouTube player that will play your video without forcing you to leave the site. You can leave a **+1**, share the video directly from the player

or continue searching for new videos in the pop-up window.

Creating your profile

Everything you share on Google+ gives the community a fuller understanding of the person you are, but to help steer opinion in the proper direction you'll want to fill in a bit about yourself in the profile section. To
access your profile page, click either your profile photo or the **profile button** in the navigation panel at the top of your page. From there you'll have the option to say more about yourself and explore all your past activity on the site.

Total control

What you see on your profile page is just about exactly what anyone who visits your Google+ site sees. You can further refine the view by clicking on any of the tabs – posts, about, photos, videos, +1's – sat just beneath the horizontal row of photos at the top of the page (assuming you've uploaded a few shots, or have a Picasa account, see p.238).

Click the **edit profile** button in the upper right of your screen and you'll be given the option of adjusting every part of your page, from adding personal information about

Edit Profile

yourself to determining who can see the people in your circles or send you an email. Hover your mouse over any section to highlight it, and click to reveal its particular set of editing and privacy options.

About you

While deciding exactly what people see when they visit your page is very useful, until you fill in some information about yourself you'll just be another disembodied voice in the social media wilderness. It's not always easy to talk about yourself, but if there's any place to start it's in the **introduction** field. Add a simple summary of who you are and, after that, listing a few

Who can see this? ⏷
- 🌐 Anyone on the web
- ⚐ Extended circles
- ◔ Your circles
- 🔒 Only you
- Custom

Click the drop-down arrow to find a number of privacy options for your posts and profile information.

skills or accomplishments in **bragging rights** might not feel entirely immodest. Details like these define and distinguish you on Google+ and are well worth the effort.

Continue developing your profile by sharing your **employment** and education history (with which Google+ will start finding connections to your classmates and coworkers), along with your gender and relationship status. If you have aliases that you go by elsewhere, including your Twitter handle (see p.114) or Tumblr name (see p.155), use the **other names** or **nickname** fields to share them – not only will this make you easier to find on Google+, but it also connects to your other presences on the web that may be more established. Lastly, if you'd like to hide your Google+ account from web searches, change **profile discovery** so that your profile is not visible to search engines.

Update your look

While still in edit mode, click **change photo** below your current profile picture to bring up a photo selection window. Upload a photo from your computer's hard drive or a Picasa album (see p.238), or take one with your computer's camera if you have one. You'll then be able to crop and reposition your photo, and use the robust set of tools inside the **creative kit** to adjust exposure and colours, or to add text, filters and effects.

The creative kit's Auto Fix feature will tweak lighting and colours to give your photos a richer tone, without you needing to fiddle with the knobs yourself.

TIP: Clicking your **profile photo** while in edit mode will flip through all the shots in your profile photos album, without taking you away from the main editing page.

Other profiles

Off to the right you'll see a place to link other social media services to Google+. This won't appear to do much but list your other accounts in the "about" portion of your profile, but in the background Google+ is using those links to determine which users you might be drawn to and whom you're most likely to influence with your own posts. You can also add any web link you'd like under the **contributor** and recommended links headings – a great way to point visitors to your online résumé or portfolio, a blog you maintain or a collaborative website of which you're a part. Completing these fields, like everything else on Google+, is completely at your desecration, but it is recommended if you're keen to strengthen your personal or business identity across the Internet.

Getting in touch

This being a *social* network, you'll probably want people to be able to contact you by **message** or **email**. Click the "send a message" or "send an email" buttons below your profile photo for the option to let one or many people contact you by these means. Enabling messages lets other people create a private post that will appear in both of your **streams**. To reply to a

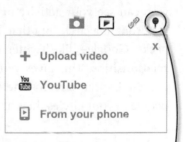

When sending a message, you're able to embed photos, videos or links alongside your text (see p.222 for more on this). You can also add your current **location** by clicking the pin icon (see p.248).

private post, simply add a **comment**. Emails are a bit more personal, and will end up in your private email account rather than showing up in the stream. But you don't need to open yourself completely – you can choose to hide your email address so that the sender can't see it outright (though they will see it once you reply to their message).

The circle game

Now that your profile is starting to take shape, you'll want to start adding friends, family and other interesting people to your **circles**. Circles are an organizing tool that let you check on and interact with specific groups of people, and at the same time limit  who can see your activity in Google+. You can add anyone you want to a circle, but that doesn't mean they must add you back – Google+, like Twitter and Tumblr, allows **asymmetric relationships**. This gives you loads more control over what you see in your stream, and may result in you having more people in your circles than have you in their's – or vice versa.

Filling in the circles

To begin the process of finding and organizing Google+ contacts, click the **circles** tab in the navigation panel at the top of your page. You'll be taken to a screen that displays all the people currently in your circles, along with some predefined circles created for you by Google+. Click the **find people** link at the top of your page and you'll  see suggestions for filling in your circles, including anyone in your email address book who may already be a member (see p.221). You can also search for any person or term in the search bar at the top of the page and add the results to a circle (see p.228).

When you've identified someone you'd like to add, simply drag their profile photo into one of the waiting family, friends, acquaintances or follow circles. Creating **new circles** is just as easy. Either drag a profile photo onto the white "drop here to create a new circle" prompt, or click that same prompt and define a new circle with or without adding members. What's more, you can add the same person to as many circles as you'd like. If, for instance, you're a member of a knitting group with your sister, you can add her to both your family circle and to one of your own creation named "knitting".

You're invited!

Though Google+ secured one hundred million users more quickly than any other social media service to date, you may find that your friends and family haven't added it to their list of must-haves just yet. If you can't find the person you're looking for within Google+, you can send an explicit invitation using the **send invitations** link on the right of your home page. A small form will open within which you can type a list of email addresses to receive your invitation. Alternatively, copy the provided link and paste it into a note to send from your regular email service. You might even consider posting this link as your status update on Facebook (see p.44), turning it into a tweet (see p.123) or sharing it on Tumblr (see p.158) to attract your friends and followers from other networks.

When you add someone to a circle, they'll receive a **notification** the next time they log in to Google+. They won't know into which circle they've been added (useful if you've placed them in "Friends who drive me crazy"), and they won't be told if you ever remove them from a circle.

> **TIP:** You can add people outside Google+ to a circle by clicking that circle, then selecting "add a new person" and entering their name and email address in the fields that pop up. These people will receive your posts via email when you share to their circle, but they will have to sign up to see your profile page.

Managing your circles

Selecting a circle will display all its members in a panel above it. From there, you can highlight one or several members and drag them into a new circle, or **remove** them en masse by clicking the link of the same name. In addition, clicking on any individual will highlight all the circles of which they're a part – not just the one you have open. And while your circles are only visible to you, that doesn't mean you can't **share a circle** as part of a post in your stream.

Katy Ball

Explore the **people who've added you** to their circles by clicking that link at the top of your circles page. Anyone you've already placed in one of your own circles will have a tiny circle icon by their name.

FindPeopleonPlus

Google+ does a fine job of suggesting people using your current connections, and their search bar returns above average results. But there's a more refined method available: http://findpeopleonplus .com will help you search the entire Google+ community using any profile field as your starting point.

Any Google+ members in the circle will receive a notification (non-Google+ members won't be revealed in the post or receive an alert), and you can choose who sees your posted circle the same way you can any of your posts (see p.224). It's also a good idea to provide a bit of description about your shared circle because its name won't be disclosed.

Deleting a circle is as simple as creating a new one, simpler even. Just click the circle and hit **delete**, but take note of the pop-up warning – people you follow who are exclusively in that circle will no longer be connected to you (if you've placed them in other circles you'll still maintain a connection), and anything you've shared with this circle in the past will no longer be visible to them.

Add to circles

Found yourself on the profile page of someone you want to follow? Simply click the **Add to circles** link on the right-hand side of their page.

TIP: If you delete a circle accidentally, you may be saved if you shared that circle. Check your stream – the deleted circle should appear in the post created when you shared it. Click the **add circle** link, and voila – your circle is restored!

Navigating the stream

The stream is the heart of your Google+ experience. This is where you'll keep up to date with all the posts shared by the people you follow, receive private messages (see p.217) and, perhaps most importantly, create your own posts to share with your followers. We touched briefly upon the stream when introducing you to your home page (see p.212), but now let's explore it in depth.

Creating posts

Even the least interesting among us come up with something worth sharing every once in a while. Before the thought slips away, click the box containing the words "share what's new…" at the top of your **home** page. The box will expand to allow you to enter text (if you lose your nerve, simply click the "×" in the upper right to close it without posting). You can also include photos, links or videos, with or without any accompanying description, by clicking the corresponding icon at the bottom of the box.

Selecting **photos** will show you choices for uploading a photo from your computer or an Android phone (see p.249) – to share a photo within any of your current Google+ albums, you'll first need to find it on your photos page, then use the options there to add it to your stream (see p.237). Sharing a **video** follows a similar pattern, with the additional option of embedding any YouTube video you find or have personally uploaded. Adding a **link** creates a short description taken from the linked web page and inserts a thumbnail image to the post. You can add further text to your link, or leave it blank and let the preview do the work for you.

Google+ hotkeys

Hotkeys make it quick and easy to move through the stream without having to push around that pesky mouse. As you browse through posts, you'll see a thin blue line on the side of the post with which you're currently engaged. You can also use some simple character cues to make your thoughts stand out within the run of text.

j	scroll down one post
k	scroll up one post
return (or enter)	open a new comment box on a highlighted post
text	bold **text**
text	italicize *text*
-text-	strikethrough ~~text~~
@ or +	directly mention a friend in your post

Narrow the focus

Google+ makes it very easy to control who can see and comment on your posts. In fact, you won't even be able to share your post unless you direct it towards at least one **circle** or individual. With the latter, simply type in an individual's name or email address and that person will be added to the list.

You can also allow all your circles to see your post, **extend** its distribution to the followers of people currently following you or leave it completely open to the **public**.

To the right of the list of names and circles with whom you're sharing is a small downward-pointing arrow, behind which is a menu with options that can restrict the conversation and spread of your post. Choosing **disable comments** will prevent other people from adding their thoughts to yours, while clicking **lock this post** stops it from being shared with anyone you hadn't originally granted access.

Once you click **share**, your post will appear in the streams of everyone you've included in your list, as well as in your own stream. When someone makes a comment it will show up under that post, and you'll be sent an alert (see p.226).

TIP: Click the arrow in the upper right-hand corner of your published posts to edit, delete or restrict outside interaction. You can also reinstate commenting and sharing features here if you've previously disabled them.

Quiet the stream

Google has created one of the most cleanly designed and easily navigable social media networks out there. But even then, constant updates coming from all corners of the web can make your stream appear a bit muddled. By default, the stream displays everyone's posts, but to help cut through the chatter you can refine whose posts you see using the power of circles.

When you form new circles, their names will appear under the **stream** header on the left of your home page. Select one of them and posts from only the members of that circle will be displayed in your stream. You'll also see the option of sharing this circle with other people (see p.220) in a link that sits on the right-hand side of the page.

Click **notifications** to see all the comments and mentions you've received in one chronological list. You can also check your notifications directly in the Google bar (see overleaf).

If people or pages have added you to their circles without you reciprocating, their posts will appear behind the **incoming** link. All incoming posts will include an "add to circles" button, in the event you deem that person or page worthy of one of your circles. Conversely, hit the **ignore** link if their posts become tedious.

The Google bar

The **Google bar**, while not exclusive to Google+, was introduced at nearly the same time that Google launched their social network. It provides an instant link to Google+ and all the other Google products, including Gmail and Google Docs (see p.236). And for something called simply a "toolbar", it has quite a bit of Google+ power built in, allowing you to create new posts and to scroll through and reply to notifications in your stream without ever leaving the webpage you're currently viewing.

Quick notifications

The Google bar appears as a black ribbon at the top of your browser window. To the left are links to a variety of Google services (see p.246), and on the right are controls specific to Google+. Whenever you're added to a new circle, earn a **+1** or receive a comment on a post, your Google bar will **notify** you with a highlighted number next to your name (the number indicates how many new notifications are waiting for your attention). Clicking the number will display brief details about each notification in a small drop-down window, and clicking any notification will open the entire post in that same tiny window. When viewing a post in this fashion, you'll be able to add new comments, edit your old comments and +1 any comment in the thread (including your own). You can also **mute** the post in case the comments won't stop coming.

Quick posts

The **share** box that sits at the top of your regular Google+ page has been condensed and added to the Google bar. Click "share.." and you'll be presented with a drop-down window that includes all the options you'd see when writing a post directly in your stream – photos, videos and links are all fair game, and you'll be able to set limits on who can comment on and share your post. Sharing outside the confines of Google+ still creates a new post in your stream, and anyone you've tagged or included will receive their alerts as usual.

When viewing your Google+ page, click the gear icon to show links to **Google+ help** and **Google+ settings**. When using other Google products, gear options will switch to help and settings for that specific service.

Click your name to reveal links to your profile and stream, plus settings for your Google account.

Search power

Social media is as much about uncovering new trends and ideas as it is about sharing your thoughts and making connections. Fortunately, Google+ is associated with the most powerful search engine on the planet – turned towards its community, that search engine can return very precise and helpful results.

Perhaps you're trying to find an interest you share with others in the Google+ community, or are eager to learn more about a current news event. Simply type your terms into the **search** box found at the top of every Google+ page, and a list of relevant people and pages will spring open. You can click one of these to be taken to that person or page's most recent posts, or if none of these instant options catches your eye, hit the enter key and you'll be taken to a page displaying more comprehensive results.

Sparks are topics that are trending across the web. They'll only show up in your searches, and are indicated by a yellow burst icon.

Here, you'll see a broad range of intermingled posts and **sparks**, but you can turn the focus to people, posts or sparks by clicking the **everything** link at the top of the list and choosing a search filter. You're able search for terms within posts made by people in your circles, or within your own posts by clicking **from everyone** and choosing the appropriate selection from the drop-down list.

You may find that you consistently search for the same terms. If that's the case, cut out a few steps by **saving your** searches. Just click "save this search" at the top of your search results screen and a link will appear on the left of your home page, underneath **what's hot** (see p.212).

> **TIP: Hashtags**, first used in Twitter (see p.126), make regular words into search terms in Google+. If you write a post and include the term #blueberries, anyone who clicks the hashtag will see a Google+ search results page for blueberries.

Reposting

Someone you know is bound to post something worthwhile on occasion – why not take the opportunity to spread it within your own circles? Sharing posts from other Google+ users is a piece of cake. Just click the **share** link under the post to send a copy to your own stream. The original author attribution remains so people can appreciate its source, and if for some reason you need to remove it you can delete it as with any other post (see p.224).

Non-public posts are considered **limited**. Click the word if you want to know who can see the post – clicking any profile photo will take you directly to that person's page.

+1's

Similar in function to Facebook's "like" button (see p.37), **+1's** let you indicate your support of a Google+ post without having to add a comment. The post's author will receive a notification of your action, though they won't be informed if you rescind your approval.

These +1 buttons are scattered all around the web – a simple click sends a note back to the **+1 tab** on your profile page (see p.214). If you've made the +1 tab visible to visitors, they can browse your interests to get a better sense of the person behind the page. The +1 tab also works as a **bookmarking** tool (see p.264). So, if you come across a great recipe on a website and give it a +1, you'll be able to find it again by checking the +1's in your Google+ profile. Do note that your +1 tab only records +1's from outside websites, it won't remember your approval of a individual's post inside Google+.

> **TIP:** Add a +1 button to your own webpage or blog by copying the code at: http://www.google.com/webmasters/+1/button

While the +1 button makes quick work of marking down things you like outside of Google+, you can also use it to create new posts without leaving the webpage you're currently viewing. Click +1, then select the **share** field to reveal an array of posting options. The result will appear in your stream as if it originated from inside Google+.

When the stream overflows

Not every post in your stream will be worth your time. In fact, the mundane will quickly overwhelm the exceptional. If you'd like to exert some control over who and what earns a place on your page, you have a few options.

Popular writers and thinkers are great people to follow when you're starting out on Google+. They'll often break stories or share interesting things about themselves and their work. But these folks tend to generate loads of +1's and comments – if you're one of those commenters be prepared for a slew of notifications alerting you to all subsequent comments. To stop the onslaught, find the original post (if you can't find it in your stream, open the **notifications** menu and click the link to the post there) and choose **mute this post** hiding beneath the small arrow in the upper right-hand corner of the post.

You can also choose to **ignore** people all together, though this option is exclusive to your incoming stream (see p.225). To stop hearing from people you've placed in circles, you can either remove them from said circles, or **block** them outright. When blocking a person, you're given the option of reporting them as well. Hopefully this isn't the case, but if they've been harassing or impersonating you, or posting inappropriate content, you may want Google to look into it for the sake of the entire community.

To reinstate a blocked or ignored person, open your circles page (see p.218), click **more options** on the right of the screen and choose the lucky person from the list.

Settings

You can control the initial spread of your posts and photos in Google+ (see p.224), and you can always remove people from your circles if they're being too noisy (see p.231), but what if you want to keep your circles as they are and still silence groups of people? Perhaps you want to maintain certain circles for sharing your own posts, but hearing back from them isn't part of the plan. If that's the case, open your **settings** and you'll find options for shuttering your comment box and turning off notifications to your phone, email and stream.

Google+ settings can be found behind the gear icon in the upper right-hand corner of any Google+ screen.

Internal interactions

As a default, actions taken by anyone within your extended circles will result in a notification, and anyone in the whole of Google+ can comment on your public posts. This means whenever a post is shared with you, or you're mentioned in a post or comment, you'll see your notification alert light up. You'll also be told when someone invites you to a **game** (see p.244) or a **hangout** (see p.234), or tags you in a **photo** (see p.239). While it is nice to know what people

+1 Sean and Frank +1'd this. Click to +1.

+1 personalization shows your name on outside sites. **Edit** Google +1 to turn it off.

are trying to share with you, over time it can become too much. Stop the unwanted alerts by limiting notifications to specific circles under the **custom** option, or cut them out all together by choosing **only you**. You have the same options for restricting comments on your public posts and for **Messenger** conversations (see the mobile section on p.251).

External notifications

You'll already have associated Google+ with an email address when you created your account. In your settings you can also add a **phone number** and decide whether you'd like to receive text messages alongside email notifications when people interact with your personal account or Google+ page. The number and scope of notification options are extensive, covering specific types of comments on posts, circles, photos and Messenger, so it's worth taking a look at these settings to ensure that you'll only be notified about events important to you, and critical to the way you use Google+.

Notifications can be sent to your email address or your mobile phone separately or simultaneously. Simply tick the appropriate box under the corresponding icon for total control over delivery.

TIP: Stop other people from freely saving your **photos** to their own computers by unticking the "allow user to download my photos" option at the bottom of your settings page.

Hanging out

Video chat isn't exclusive to Google+ (see p.50), but considering the quality and features available in their video **hangouts**, you may end up moving all your video correspondence to the service. It's a fun way to keep in touch with friends and  family who live far away, and just as useful for business meetings between coworkers and clients in different cities. Best of all – it's completely free.

Click **start a hangout** on the right of your home page to open your hangout inside a new browser window (you may be asked to install a plug-in – go ahead and do it). After you've fixed your hair and tested your microphone, give your hangout a name and choose which circles or individuals you'd like to invite – you can invite as many people as you'd like, but only ten people can be in the hangout at once. People who join can invite other people as well, so there's a chance that your casual chat could evolve into something else entirely.

Every Google+ hangout comes with a toolbar, where you'll see controls to manage your interactions with the group. Here you'll find buttons to turn your video and audio feed off and on, invite new people, open a text chat with the group, search for and share YouTube videos, and use highly sophisticated facial recognition software to attach fake moustaches under everyone's noses.

Google Chat

If you have a Gmail account, you'll already be familiar with Google Chat – Google's take on instant messaging. In Google+ you'll see a **chat** option to the left of your screen with about a dozen names underneath. Coloured icons indicate whether these people are online, busy or set up for **video**. If you don't see the name of the person with whom you'd like to chat, type it into the search field (below which you can set your own status) or sign out of chat completely, by clicking the tiny drop-down arrow.

Selecting a name opens a small box in the lower corner of your screen where you can exchange notes. Add **emoticons** to your text by clicking the smiley face in the lower right corner of the text box, or start a voice or video chat by clicking the video and phone icons, respectively. You can also make the chat box open in a new window with the upward pointing arrow in the upper right – very useful for keeping a chat active while navigating away from your Google+ page.

Reopening a closed chat window will let you pick up your conversation right where you left off. If you don't want Google to record your chats, choose **go off the record** under the actions menu. Here, you'll also find an option to **share files** across chat.

You'll see all the participants organized into a strip of tiny moving images. As people talk, their image will be promoted to the large screen. The constant switching is sometimes jarring, so you may want to click on an individual to manually promote them to the main window. Clicking a person will also give you the choice of **muting** them.

Video chat is great for talking out ideas, and with the integration of **notes** and **sketchpad** it makes real-time collaboration a snap. Click the notes icon to open a new text document that anyone in your hangout can add to, or use the sketchpad to create images and designs that will help illuminate ideas and projects. You can also share any saved

 file in your **Google Docs** folders, or turn your camera off and share your computer screen with the hangout instead (very useful for running a presentation or describing how to use software).

When you're ready to leave, just click **exit** and the window will disappear. In case the name of a person you just met slips your mind (it happens, especially if other people start adding friends), check your stream – you'll find a new post listing all the people with whom you've just hung out.

TIP: In the event that your camera or microphone isn't working properly, click the **settings** button and you'll be given a series of cues to test parts of your system. One thing it won't check is if you're playing music – a common cause of confused microphones!

Photos

Considering how easy it is to add a photo to any post (see p.222), it should come as no surprise that managing your albums and browsing your friends' photos is similarly straightforward – though there is a quirk of organization that could cause a stumble now and then.

Get organized

Your photos exist in two distinct places in Google+. The first is on your profile page (see p.214), under the tab for **photos**. Here you'll see albums full of images you've attached to your posts, your set of profile photos and any albums you've previously created in Picasa (see overleaf) – any albums you don't see on this page exist behind the link that reads "view all of your albums". You'll also have access to photos in which you've been tagged (either by yourself or other Google+ users).

You can add photos to any current album by clicking that album to open it, then choosing to add more photos. Or you may want to create an entirely **new album** – easily managed

◻️⁺ ADD MORE PHOTOS

by clicking the **upload new photos** button, entering an album name, then dragging as many photos as you'd like into the upload box before hitting **create album**. You'll also

Picasa

Before Google+ was Picasa – Google's web-based photo management tool. Using the same clean interface and drag-and-drop interactivity that makes all of Google's offerings so appealing, **Picasa** makes it easy for you to arrange your photos and share them with friends and family. It also has a downloadable component that will sit in your computer and help you quickly upload groups of photos. But now, just about everything you could do in Picasa is available in Google+, meaning you're able to create and edit **albums**, store them online and share them with your **circles** from the comfort of one account. This doesn't mean you need to swap one for the other – Picasa is still useful if you don't want to completely submerge yourself in Google+'s stream.

If you're already a Picasa user, your photo albums will automatically appear on your Google+ photos page (with the privacy features you selected in Picasa). If you aren't, and would like to get an account, head to http://picasa.google.com and step through the sign up process. As a reward for being a Google+ user, you'll be allowed to have larger files and longer videos than non-Google+ users. You'll also be able to follow people on Picasa who haven't joined Google+, make **collages**, **slideshows** and order physical **prints** right on the site. And while you can use the search bar to find photos in Google+, Picasa will show you a list by subject next to the fun little guessing game "Where in the World?".

have the chance to name the people in your photos: Google+ will use its facial recognition abilities to find individuals in your photos then ask you to **tag** them. In future uploads, they'll suggest tagging the same people automatically. As a last step you'll be asked if you'd like to share your new (or updated) album with people in your stream. Neither tagging nor posting is mandatory, and they're both simple enough to **skip**, using the button of the same name.

> **TIP:** Any **videos** you add to your posts will show up under the videos tab in your profile page. Each one will be represented as an individual album, and you can manage them with the same set of features available for photo albums.

The second place your photos are kept is behind the photos tab in the **navigation bar** at the top of every Google+ page. You'll see all the same photos here that you saw in your profile, plus photos uploaded by everyone in your circles (including shared photos from their Picasa accounts) and any photos uploaded automatically from your smartphone's mobile app (see p.247).

Stop your shots from being shared outside your own circles by using the **lock** options found at the top of each picture or album.

Interact

When you click on any photo in your albums, it will open in a black-backed window along with a whole new set of options. You can tag yourself or others (other people will be sent an alert and given the chance to approve the tag before it goes live), add **comments** which will be appended to the photo in your stream and delete, share, download or edit the photo. You'll also see a strip of thumbnails along the bottom of the page that includes all the images in the active album. Click any thumbnail to enlarge that photo, or use the dimmed arrows to the left and right of the main photo to move through the choices.

Editing options for photos are particularly powerful in Google+. You won't be able to edit another user's photos (unless you download it first and save it back into a personal album), but to readjust your own, click the **edit** button in the lower left corner. Here you'll see options to rotate your photos or **auto-fix** the colour and lighting. If you prefer a more hands-on approach, open the creative kit, within which you'll have many more editing choices, including a cropping tool and effects overlays (see p.216).

When you're done, add a **caption** to the bottom of the image and exit the page by clicking the white "×" in the upper right-hand corner of the photo. You'll be taken back to the album your photo is in – hover your mouse over an image to reveal any captions.

Pages

If you maintain a website, run a small (or large) business or lead a group, you'll want to promote it with a **page**. Pages are very similar to regular Google+ accounts, but they do have a few important differences – mainly in the  way you can interact with people and disseminate your messages. And while the overall features of Google+ are sure to be adjusted from time to time, it's in the pages that we're bound to see the most innovation.

Make your page

Click the "create a page" link on the right of your home screen and you'll be given a few choices to help define what sort of page you're creating. If you find that your particular endeavour isn't represented, you may also choose "other". Now provide some information about your page, making sure to include your website if you have one (you can also

CONVERSATIONBUDDY   PROFILEBUDDY   CONVERSIONBUDDY   ANALYTICSBUDDY

Buddy Media, a social media marketing firm whose smartphone app can help you schedule posts and keep track of your Google+ page's analytics, uses the photos in their **scrapbook** album to help personalize their profile page.

use a **Tumblr** site, see p.149), then choose whether to make your page visible to any Google+ user, or restrict access by age. You must tick the box labelled "I agree to the pages terms and I am authorized to create this page" before hitting that **create** button – but remember, Google is quite strict about their terms and will not hesitate to delete your page if you misrepresent yourself.

> **TIP:** If photos and videos aren't something you need (or want) to share with potential customers, you can remove those tabs from your profile page. While editing your profile (see p.214), click either "photos" or "videos" and adjust the visibility accordingly.

Attracting attention

Once you've created your page, you'll use Google+ the same way as when you're logged into your personal profile. You can comment, post and add +1's, start **hangouts**, upload photos – all in your page's name. The only difference lies in your **circles**. In order to stop companies from sending out spam to large groups of people, you'll only be able to put people in your page's circles who have already added you to one of their own circles. You'll also notice that the default circles are different from those for

Click the "spread the word" link to the right of your page's stream, and you'll create a new post from your personal Google+ account letting all your friends know about your new page.

your personal account. Here, VIPs, **customers** and team members have replaced family, friends and acquaintances. The concept behind circles is the same, but now you'll want to create circles of consumers to send pointed messages and product alerts to.

When you want to return to your personal page, or if you need to make a comment on someone's page as yourself rather than your business, simply click the arrow that appears under your page name and select the word **you**. This reloads Google+ with your personal settings, photos, posts and circles. You can return to your page at any time using the same drop-down arrow.

> **TIP:** When your page is new you aren't likely to have many followers. To hide your unpopularity, navigate to your page's profile, click "change who is visible here" in the left-hand column and deselect the option for displaying the people who have you in their circles. Once your number comes up you can reinstate it.

Google is known for their analytical tools – ways for you to track who visits a website and for what purpose. In Google+ they've enabled **ripples**, which give you the ability to track the spread of any public post over time. Just click the word **public** next to any post and you'll be able to see the entire share thread.

Jaana Nyström

Jaana Nyström Inskkolaste church Mika Usuru Funk Yamazaki Chris Wilson Paul Simbeck-Hampson Huy Daniel

Chris Wilson   Paul Simbeck-Hampson

Games

When you're out of things to talk about in your hangouts (see p.234) or at a loss for words to post, it may be time to take a break and head for the **games** section of the site. Some games are collaborative, while most will just pit you against other

players (or at least compare your high scores). Let's take a look at some of the time-wasting features built into Google+.

Share the fun

Click the **games** button at the top of your Google+ home page to load a window of featured games. A slideshow will scroll through all the top games, and as each one fills the page you'll see who among your friends have played that game recently. When you find a game you want to try, click the icon and a screen will pop up asking for permission to look in your circles to see who might also be playing that game. These games are intended to be **social experiences**, and while the games' makers may take note of your age, gender and other information about you, they're not supposed to use it irresponsibly or sell it to a third party.

Recently played

 Diamond Dash

 Angry Birds

 Zynga Poker

Any game you **recently played** will be recorded in an easily accesable list on the left of your screen. Tap any icon to immediately launch the game.

Most games on Google+ currently exist in some form elsewhere, though there are a few unique features that encourage cooperation with the people in your circles. For instance, Angry Birds on Google+ is almost the same as Angry Birds on your iPad, though in the former there are **teamwork** levels that allow you to play with other Google+ members. Most games will make it obvious if there's a cooperative or competitive component - search in the game to find an option to invite a friend or join a group. Notifications of game invitations will appear along with other regular Google+ **notifications**, as well as on the game page.

The games stream

Below the featured games on the main games page is your **games stream** – the place where any activity you share from within games will be displayed. If you want to brag about your latest online poker winnings or the number of orcs you've slain, go ahead - you won't see it in your personal stream.

The games stream will also display invitations to play games with people in your circles, as well as links to help friends collect bonuses or prizes. You can take more of a supporting role by commenting

Some games will encourage you to buy add-ons or upgrades. Any virtual transactions are handled by **Google checkout** and are funded by credit or debit card.

on, sharing or leaving a +1 on games posts. But if you do, your comment will leave the game stream and be posted in your personal stream, where people and circles outside the game can see it.

If you ever want to remove a game's access to your personal account information, navigate to that game and look under its window to find a tiny arrow next to the game's name. Click that and select **manage permissions**. You'll be taken to a page listing every service currently connected with all your Google accounts. Choose the one you want to cut off, and click **revoke access**. Privacy restored.

Google Reader

We've seen how Google+ has integrated YouTube, Picasa and Google Docs as part of its services, but the changes aren't so one-sided. You can +1 and comment right in YouTube and Picassa to send posts back to your stream, and the same goes for **Google Reader** – Google's news aggregator (see p.266 for more on aggregators).

As you surf the web, you may come across news items, authors or subjects you'd like to keep track of. Rather than searching for those people and things every day, automate the process using Google Reader. Head to www.google.com/reader and type in search terms for Reader to find. You can also click the orange **RSS icon** next to any article or page as your browse the web and Reader will remember those terms. To share your finds back on Google+, simply click +1 or share.

Google+ mobile

With Google having developed Android (their own smartphone operating system), it stands to reason that they'd also create a smartphone application for Google+. You can check your phone's app store for a version, or go to www.google.com/mobile/+ and see if your phone is supported. Once you download the mobile app, you'll be able to share photos, join hangouts, add comments and do many other things possible in the web version of Google+ directly from your mobile.

> **TIP:** If your phone doesn't have a Google+ app yet, but can still access the Internet, use your phone's web browser to visit m.google.com/app/plus. Here you'll see a version of the site optimized for your tiny mobile screen.

Stream

The stream in the mobile app behaves in much the same way as it does on the full Google+ website. Tapping its icon will take you to a list of all the recent posts from your combined circles. Swipe the screen from left to right to scroll through other **stream views**, including one called **nearby** – a circle exclusive to the mobile app that will show you all the public posts made within a few miles of your current location. You can add additional stream views by adding circles to your stream in your mobile settings (see p.252). Select any post to leave a **comment** or give it a +1, or click the tiny arrow next to the comment box to reveal options that will let you

share, mute or report the post. You're also able to create your own **posts** in the stream, and attach photos or videos taken from your phone, by clicking the pencil icon in the upper right of the screen.

Tap **notifications** at the bottom of the app window to reveal a list of current and past alerts. Tap any notification to be brought directly to that post, comment or tag.

Checking in

Let people know where you are by tapping the **checkmark** icon at the top of the stream. You'll be brought to a screen listing every business and public location in your general vicinity. Choose where you are, write a note about what you're doing and post it to your stream – it will show up immediately in both your mobile stream and the one back on the web. If you don't see the place you're looking for, try searching for it by name. You won't be able to add a **venue** to the list though, and you won't be getting any fancy badges for check-ins, as with location-based service **FourSquare**.

Managing circles

The **circles icon** on the mobile home page will take you to a list of people in your circles, which you can swap for a global view of all your current circles. You can create a new circle from that page, or open any current circle to see posts and photos from its members.

If you come across someone you'd like to put in a circle, tap their name to be brought to their profile page, where you'll see a button to **add** them. Click it and you'll be able to include them in an existing circle or create a new circle just for them. Anyone already in a circle won't have the add button – instead, you'll see the circles of which they're currently a part. Tapping those will let you add them to more circles, or delete them from their current circles.

Sharing photos

Behind the photo icon is a set of **albums** that will look very similar to the ones in the web version of Google+. Tapping an album containing photos from your circles will let you make a comment

Tap the **camera icon** to take a picture with your phone's camera and post it to your stream. Alternatively, you can click the **album icon** next to it and pick one in your camera roll.

on any of them, which will in turn send a notification to the owner of that photo. Open your own albums to scroll through your entire collection of pics (including any that are shared with Picasa, see p.238). You can add comments to any of these photos, turn one into your **profile picture** or tap the tiny arrow by its comment field to delete it from the album. You can also browse through photos from your phone

Click the many boxes icon in the upper left to be taken back to your home screen.

and select sets of them to post to your stream. Any pictures you choose from your phone will end up in your "photos from your posts" album in Google+.

TIP: Android smartphone users will have the option of instant uploads – any photo or video you take will be automatically backed up in a private Google+ album named "Photos from your phone", found on the web version's photo page.

Messenger

The **messenger** feature enables private instant messaging between two or more Google+ app users. Tap the messenger icon and you'll be brought to a screen showing all your active conversations. Create a new message by tapping the small messenger icon in the upper right, then add a name, email address or circle to the conversation. Your first message starts the chat and sends an alert to the mobile phones of everyone you've invited (but only to their mobile phones – messenger is exclusive to the mobile app). While waiting for a reply, you can **name** the conversation by selecting the gear icon in the top right of the conversation window, or add more people from your circles by clicking the tiny +people icon. If you tire of the current thread, the gear icon is also where you'll find options to **leave** the conversation or **mute** it so you stop receiving notifications about it on your phone.

> **TIP:** Touch the arrow at the top of any conversation and you'll be given the option of creating a new circle from all the people currently included in that message thread.

Video chats

While it is possible for you to join **hangouts** from the mobile app (assuming your smartphone has a built-in camera and you're on a Wi-Fi network), you currently can't begin one from your mobile phone – only from the Google+ website. If someone invites you to a hangout, you'll see an alert in your notifications bar, and from there you can join, but not invite anyone new. Considering how common public mobile phone chatter has become, video chat won't affect the people around you too much, but you'd do well to check your surroundings to ensure you don't reveal some side of yourself better left undisclosed.

Mobile settings

There are a number of **SMS** alerts, controlled through the web version of Google+, that will help you stay within touching distance of your account (see p.233). But those with the mobile app have a whole other set of choices. To begin, tap the **gear** icon in the upper left corner of your home page. You'll see a button that will sign you out of the app, and beneath that will be the choice of managing **push notifications**. These are the same SMS notifications that you can adjust on your Google+ webpage. They control what sort of activity in your stream should result in your receiving a text message – from mentions and shares to comments and tags.

The remaining options deal exclusively with how your mobile app performs. Tap **stream views** to choose which circles you can see in your stream page – those with green checks will appear in order from left to right (see p.247). And if you'd rather not converse with certain people, click under **messenger** to limit who can invite you to join a conversation.

Tap and hold the icon opposite any circle, and you'll be able to drag it into a different display order.

Peripherals

Peripherals
Sites worth knowing

Over the course of this book we've taken a close look at the biggest and most popular social media services out there, but there are many smaller, more focused services that provide things the big guys haven't gotten right just yet. And while we don't delve so deeply into these services as we did elsewhere, most are so focused that their features and functions will be obvious. If you've been able to successfully navigate through Facebook, these will be a piece of cake.

None of the following services want to know every little thing about you – they don't care whom you're related to or when you graduated from college. Some, like the aggregates, don't even care who you are; they just want to help you bring the rush of web content under control. A few desire nothing more than to bring people together in person after they've met online, while others exist solely as repositories for your photos and home videos. What all of these have in common is that they will enhance your connection with social media for the better. Why not try a few out?

Events

Inspired no doubt by the flash-mob craze, the Internet is becoming *the* way for groups of all kinds to self-identify and get together, either virtually or face to face. No matter how obscure your interest may be, there is almost certainly a group on the Internet for you. Several sites are devoted to putting like-minded people together, and have become instrumental in social movements of all descriptions.

Meetup (www.meetup.com)

With a wide reach and simple interface, Meetup is currently the most popular social media event organizer available. When you join, you simply provide information about the kinds of  things you like, from very general (music) to the mind-numbingly specific (Korean pop), type in your **location**, and you'll be shown an array of local meetups on the left of the screen, matched to a calendar on the right. Meetup plays very nicely with **Facebook** – let it turn on Facebook Connect (see p.81) and one click will load your Facebook friends' activities into your Meetup home page.

You can also organize your own group by clicking **start a group** at the top of the page. Ideally, you'll want to start with some people already lined up to join, but there is a strong "if you build it, they will come" ethos within the service. There are a few keys to being a successful **organizer**. First, while your passion for the topic of the group should be evident and hopefully inspiring, don't necessarily count on every member to share the depth of your enthusiasm. Second, **communicate**! Let people know about events, and make sure you show up to them. Finally, should your group grow exponentially, off-load some of the responsibilities to **assistant organizers**. Meetup even offers occasional organizer boot camps (which you can attend in person or online) to help answer questions.

Songkick (www.songkick.com)

Songkick is similar to Meetup, but specific to **live music** aficionados. Users work together to build up a massive database of every concert ever performed, including information on the venue, set lists, band lineups and even bootleg **multimedia**. Songkick also wants you to note who has been attending the shows you have, and add them as a friend. The goal is to make concert attending something that extends beyond the event itself. With enough user feedback, Songkick hopes to become the IMDB of live music, creating a historical archive for researchers as well as enthusiasts.

Yahoo! users have their own internal events network with the upcoming.yahoo.com site – a shared calendar tailored to fit your personal and group interests.

Entertainment

While activities like watching television or DVDs can seem a solitary pursuit, lots of people enjoy adding a social dimension to the mix. Services like **Miso** (http://gomiso.com) and **TV.com Relay** (http://tv.com/relay) alert friends to the television show or movie you're watching, and let you share comments and critiques across your Internet connection. This allows you to interact with a community of viewers, in real time, from the comfort of your own home.

GetGlue (http://getglue.com)

Currently, the most popular of these services is **GetGlue**. On sign up you provide a sense of what genres you like by picking from a number of popular shows, and as you develop your profile GetGlue will recommend new shows and films based on your preferences. You can **follow** people to discover content through their likes and dislikes, and you can find and add friends from Twitter and Facebook. GetGlue offers virtual **stickers** to its users (hence their name) to encourage you to participate in conversations with users across the community. Earn enough stickers and you'll be bestowed with the status of **guru**.

Miso (http://gomiso.com) has a robust database of film and television shows that you can explore, and their user interface is intuitive and elegant. They also have a smartphone app that makes sharing comments and downloading iTunes shows possibly too easy…

Shopping

Group-buying through social coupon sites has exploded over the past couple of years, most notably with **Living Social** (www.livingsocial.com) and **Groupon** (www.groupon.com). Merchants propose a deal for goods or services through one of these portals, and if enough subscribers sign up to purchase the deal, an e-coupon is generated, often with significant savings. While there isn't usually direct interaction between members, it is their combined effort that makes it all work.

> **TIP:** Subscribing to a social coupon aggregator may be a smart option. Sites like **Yipit**, **Cake Deal** or **DealSurf** provide subscribers with all the deals in their area, including **Groupon**, **Living Social** and dozens more.

Putting a touch more "social" into social buying is **Blippy** (http://blippy.com), where subscribers share reviews about what they're buying, independent of any one service that controls both the goods and the comments (like Amazon.com). You can sign in with your Facebook account so you'll be immediately connected to everyone you know, and (for the more trusting among us) let Blippy scan your Gmail account for receipts to create a queue of purchases awaiting your description. You can even sync iTunes and eBay accounts to create automatic posts from your purchases.

Photos

Photo sharing used to be an amazingly cumbersome enterprise. Digitization, and the utter ubiquity of cameras, has changed all that. Sharing and storing images is simple, straightforward – and, best of all, virtually free! While it is still your job to shoot the picture, name it and upload it, photo hosting services make organizing and sharing photos easier than ever.

Flickr

Flickr is quite easy to use, and will helpfully give new users tips on organizing photos into **albums** and searching your archive by topic, camera used and **geographic location**. Ordering **prints** through the website is simple, and while Flickr has some monthly limits on the number of pictures you can upload, only the most compulsive photo takers will run into trouble. If you're one of them, a small annual fee provides unlimited storage. Sharing photos with other Flickr users is a piece of cake, and while anyone with an account can explore your public shots, you can close your albums to all but a few people you specifically invite.

TIP: If you want to share photos with a group of people outside Flickr, send them a guest pass with the **share this** button.

Picasa

Being affiliated with Google can be a blessing and a curse. Picasa is a powerful program, and its integration with **Google+** makes it very attractive for members of both sites. But your photos can easily show up on Google search, which is great if you're trying to drive traffic to your site, and possibly annoying otherwise. For more on Picasa, see p.238.

Instagram

The mobile phone has made picture-taking an everyday activity for millions, and while you can upload photos from your phone to Facebook, it'd be nice to do a bit of touching up before passing it along in raw form. Enter, **Instagram**.

First, Instagram is a camera app, providing a series of filters and effects that can make your photos sing. Second, it is a social network built around sharing pictures. You can send your shots to Facebook or Twitter as well, but Instagram has it's own dedicated network of photogs. Pop a few shots, work out some captions and hit **post** to share them with your Instagram pals. You can browse the network of users and add people you want to follow right from your phone, or search your address book for people who are already part of the service. The community is generally encouraging and supportive, so don't be shocked if you hear some comments about those great shots you put up from your last holiday!

Video sharing

The emergence of digital video has made sharing and viewing videos easier than sharing photographs used to be in the Dark Ages (like the 1970s!). With no more than a reasonably smart phone, you can shoot a video, upload it and share it with the world – or just your friends and family – in minutes.

YouTube

YouTube may have been developed to make sharing personal videos among friends less cumbersome, but it has become so much more. Alongside its integration with Google+, it now houses full-length movies and television shows, and even streams live events. This has made YouTube a great hangout, as well as a place where **subscribers** to your **channel** can view your original work. Although YouTube is a fairly open system and virtually anyone can stumble across a video you share, you can mark your videos as **unlisted** so they won't appear in general searches. Unlisted videos have their own unique URLs that you can send to whomever you choose – though nothing stops people from passing them on.

Vimeo, another major video sharing service, attracted their first users thanks to their emphasis on high video quality and their sophisticated interface, making them the favourite of the more technologically advanced videographer.

Books

The folks who feared that the Internet would render book reading irrelevant need only look at the popularity of book-oriented sites like **Goodreads**, **Shelfari** and **LibraryThing** to realize that the web has helped bring a community of bibliophiles together. Stressing two main functions – cataloguing and reviewing – these sites encourage and enhance the reading experience of millions of people across the world.

LibraryThing has an academic, professional air about it, and is mostly focused on helping you keep track of what you've read – though you can also build a friend network and check out your friends' libraries.

Goodreads

The most social of the bookcentric sites, Goodreads helps users build a network of like-minded readers to share literature reviews. You'll see everyone's reading activity on your home page and be given the opportunity to set up public and private **book clubs**. You can easily add books to your profile, sorting them into three categories: currently reading, read and to-read. Members are encouraged to rate books and offer brief reviews before browsing friends' lists to find their next book. Further enhancing the social experience, Goodreads offers thousands of groups for members to join, giving members a chance to dig deeper into unfamiliar genres and to discover new authors.

Bookmarking

You're probably familiar with creating a bookmark in your browser – useful for remembering sites you've visited and stories you've read online. **Social bookmarking** encourages users to describe and share their bookmarks in a much more public and interconnected way, and in the process help develop a large collaborative taxonomy of web content. Let's take a look at the most popular services.

Digg

Digg's mission is to connect people all over the world through similar interests, and to provide searchers with information from the web that has been refracted through the lens of the Digg community (who **vote** on links, helping to create a certain level of quality control). You can follow other users and be alerted to what they've "dug", or check out stories from **my news** – a personalized selection of articles created by Digg based on your profile and activity. Simply sign up, then click the **digg** link next to articles you read and enjoy on the web.

Reddit helps you manage links to articles, images and video. Users can share stories, or browse within Reddit's networks or sub-networks ("sub-reddits", naturally). Coming under some fire for its libertarian stance that has seen the proliferation of a number of adult-related sub-reddits,Reddit is unusually eclectic in its offerings.

StumbleUpon

An add-on to your browser, StumbleUpon captures the joy of diving headlong into the myriad rabbit holes found on the web. While users can search by tags or subjects, there is also an option called **stumbling**, which can take you almost anywhere. They have managed to make one of the most daunting elements of the information explosion – the vastness of what's out there – fun, by applying an almost childlike whimsy to the search experience.

Pinterest.com has taken the idea of a pinboard – a corkboard where you can tack up article clippings and pictures that inspire you (or that you want to remember to buy, share or otherwise not forget) – and have recreated it on the web. A click of their "pin it" button will save anything you find while browsing online back to your board. You'll also see friends' pins, and be able to comment on and share them à la Facebook.

Delicious

Owned and managed by the originators of **YouTube**, Delicious has a feature unique to their bookmarking service called stacks. While you can skip around the web collecting bookmarks as with the other services mentioned above, **stacks**

allow you to collect a number of links and group them thematically. Then, when interacting with your friends in the network, you can share individual links or entire stacks with them.

Content aggregators

After reading this book, you may find yourself with a bunch of social media accounts all wanting your attention. Why not bring them under one roof with a **content aggregator**? These tools, including **Paper.li**, **Zite** and **Read It Later**, help organize all the content coming your way in one place so you don't have to jump from site to site to site to find out what's happening in all your virtual social worlds.

Flipboard

Available for smartphones and **tablets**, Flipboard takes material from your Facebook and Twitter streams, along with stories from your favourite websites, and reformats them into a really lovely magazine layout. Rather than reading a **tweet** with a link attached, Flipboard shows the tweet and a little snippet of the article or image behind the link. Click any story fragment, and the whole article will open in a dedicated page. Moving away from long lists of alerts and updates into this visually appealing format can help you remember what reading was like before the web.

If this then that (www.ifttt.com) is an idea based in computer programming – if one action happens, then execute this other command. Thanks to this service, you can apply conditional operations to Facebook, Twitter, email, calendars, instant messaging, the weather…the list goes on.

Index

Index